food for
family & friends

food for
family & friends

simply delicious recipes for stylish
entertaining at home

RYLAND
PETERS
& SMALL

LONDON NEW YORK

Senior Designer Steve Painter
Senior Commissioning Editor Julia Charles
Picture Researcher Emily Westlake
Production Toby Marshall
Art Director Leslie Harrington
Publishing Director Alison Starling

Indexer Hilary Bird

First published in the United Kingdom
in 2011
by Ryland Peters & Small
20–21 Jockey's Fields
London WC1R 4BW
www.rylandpeters.com

10 9 8 7 6 5 4 3 2 1

Text © Fiona Beckett, Emily Chalmers, Ross
Dobson, Tonia George, Louise Pickford, Ben Reed
and Ryland Peters & Small 2011.

Design and photographs
© Ryland Peters & Small 2011

ISBN: 978 1 84975 122 3

A catalogue record for this book
is available from the British Library.

Printed and bound in China.

Notes

• All spoon measurements are level unless
otherwise specified.

• Eggs are medium unless otherwise specified.
Uncooked or partially cooked eggs should not
be served to the very old, frail, young children,
pregnant women or those with compromised
immune systems.

• When a recipe calls for the zest of citrus fruit,
buy unwaxed fruit and wash well before using. If
you can only find treated fruit, scrub well in warm,
soapy water before using.

• Ovens should be preheated to the specified
temperature. Recipes in this book were tested
using a regular oven. If using a fan-assisted oven,
follow the manufacturer's instructions for adjusting
temperatures.

Contents

Secrets of successful entertaining

For many people entertaining is stressful. We invite family, friends, work colleagues or neighbours round on impulse, then wish we hadn't. We leave thinking about the event until the last minute, try something too complicated, then panic. But it really doesn't need to be like that. It's easy to lose sight of the main reason for having a gathering, which is to enjoy yourself and to make sure your guests have a good time. All too often your worries about what food to serve become such an overriding concern that you end up completely stressed and worn out. The good news, though, is that it's never been easier to entertain without spending hours cooking or spending a fortune on caterers. These days you can buy in many of the things you will need, such as canapés, platters of cold meats or seafood, salads and cheeseboards. You can then concentrate on preparing the dishes you do best or most enjoy making. What you also need to do is to focus on what sort of party you want, and ask yourself a few questions.

First, what sort of occasion is it? Do you want to celebrate in style or simply get a few friends together? Do you want it to be an occasion that everyone will remember or just a relaxed affair? Next, have you got the space to invite as many people as you want to and to throw the sort of party you have in mind within your budget? Do you have the time – or the skill – to prepare the sort of meal you're planning? For example, if you've never cooked for more than four friends before, you might find cooking for eight daunting without help. If so, how are you going to get round that? Get professional help? Buy in ready-made dishes? Enlist help from family and friends? If you're going to make part of the food yourself, don't leave yourself too many things that require last-minute attention or embark on recipes that you've never attempted before.

Planning the menu is the next thing to consider. Styles of food and quantities required will vary depending on the age and sex of your guests (younger guests and men tending to eat more than older guests and women). As a general rule, allow six to eight nibbles per person for a drinks party, of which one or two could be sweet, and one and a half servings in total of any main course, two servings of salad or vegetables and two of dessert, on the assumption that a third to a half of your guests will come back for a second helping. If you want to limit the amount that your guests eat, don't offer too many options, as people like to try everything, especially desserts! Remember to check if there is anything your guests can't eat – food intolerances are quite common these days, so it's wise to check in advance.

Consider the drinks you serve. The more different types of drink you offer, the more your guests will drink and the more glasses they'll use. A choice of two types of wine, two different soft drinks and water is plenty, although you can obviously lay on an aperitif or cocktail, and one or two beers and jug drinks for a summer party, if you wish. A reasonable amount to cater for is half a bottle of wine per head, although if a do is likely to go on for quite a time or you have guests who are likely to drink rather more than that, allow a bottle each in total.

Good choices for a drinks party are Champagne or sparkling wine or a light, refreshing white and a soft, fruity red. (Avoid wines that are heavily oaked or high in alcohol, which can easily result in your guests drinking more than they realize and can also make them uncomfortably hot and flushed.) As a general rule, you'll probably need twice as much white wine as red. For an event with hot food, you need wines with a little more weight – consult the Wine with Food chapter (see pages 176–185) for the individual dishes you're planning to serve. Either way, it's best to go for wines that everyone will enjoy; ideal choices would be lighter styles of Chardonnay and Sauvignon Blanc for the whites and soft reds such as Merlot or Pinot Noir. If you're holding an outdoor event like a barbecue, you could easily serve rosé instead of a white and pink fizz is also great fun too.

The final thing to consider is equipment. It's rare to have enough glasses, plates and cutlery to cater for a crowd, so make sure you hire or borrow enough for everyone. Many wine shops and supermarkets now offer glass hire – play safe and allow two wine glasses per head. If you're organizing a brunch, barbecue or any other event that requires special equipment (such as juicers or outdoor grills), again, make sure you have a sufficient number to avoid long delays in producing the food or drinks. Finally, and most importantly, relax and enjoy yourself!

setting the scene

Table setting used to be a very formal affair, with strict rules and regulations for every occasion. Tableware reflected status, and thus presenting it correctly was a key social skill. Today, entertaining has become far more relaxed and we have happily abandoned all the pomp and circumstance. That said, setting the table for lunch with friends or a celebratory family dinner shouldn't be a chore or an afterthought. Creating a decorative tabletop is easy, satisfying and fun, and even the simplest scheme will have a transforming effect on the atmosphere of any occasion – and on your guests. The next few pages offer plenty of ideas to inspire you, whether you are having a simple tapas party with friends or celebrating Mother's Day with a special meal. Remember, successful table dressing is not about silver spoons or fine crystal; it's about making the most of what you have and adding a memorable, personal touch.

Table linens

Many of us today do without tablecloths and even napkins, but these offer the perfect finishing touch for a meal. Both practically and aesthetically, using a tablecloth makes sense.

It will protect the tabletop from heat or scratches, reduce noise and limit breakages. Most importantly, a tablecloth can give a very average table the air of something smarter – even a wobbly old trestle looks impressive when topped with a lovely cloth. Linen used to be the must-have material (hence the generic name), but these days tablecloths come in many different guises: printed cotton, heavy damask and vinyl-coated cloth. Choose something that will suit the occasion. Delicate white linen may be just the thing for a vintage tea, but wouldn't be right for a children's party. Here, vinyl-coated cloth is perfect as it's cheap, cheerful and easy to clean. You don't even need a proper cloth, just buy enough metres of fabric to fit your table.

According to the rules of etiquette, tablecloth overhang should measure 15–20 cm for breakfast or lunch and 20–30 cm or more for dinner, but how many of us are really going to get out the ruler? Just use your common sense; an average overhang of about a foot or so is fine, whatever the occasion. An undercloth (sometimes called a silence cloth or a table pad) can help to make the top cloth drape properly and will also provide extra protection against hot dishes. To make your own, buy suitable material online or just cut an old blanket down to size.

You don't need to spend a fortune on a new tablecloth. Keep your eyes open at car boot sales or antiques markets for old linen cloths or sheets, or consider using something more unusual. An old curtain could make an inspired cloth; a swathe of Eastern-style fabric provide the perfect backdrop for an oriental meal. Alternatively, top the table with lengths of wallpaper or pieces of wrapping paper for a one-off occasion. The paper will look graphic and interesting, and – even better – it won't need washing!

If you want your tabletop left on show, opt for a runner rather than a cloth. These come in countless colours and textures, and will bring a chic modern look to your tabletop. Invest in placemats and napkins to match, if you like, or choose some in contrasting colours and textures for a more decorative effect.

Dinnerware

It wasn't all that long ago that owning a smart dinner service was essential. Saved-up for piece by piece or given as a present, this staple of the wedding list was a treasured possession, only brought out on special occasions.

Today, entertaining is a much more informal affair, and keeping fine china 'just for best' seems a wasteful concept. Now that we are far more likely to have friends round for a relaxed kitchen supper than to serve a formal dinner in the dining room, we need dinnerware we can use whatever the occasion.

If you are starting a collection from scratch, you don't need to spend a huge amount of money. Choose a good basic service that you can use every day and dress up for parties; a simple design or plain colour will give you most flexibility when it comes to dressing the table. Plain white china is hard to beat. Not only does it set food off perfectly, but it goes with everything else on the table, too. Add pattern and texture in placemats, coasters or tablecloths to make the setting more visually interesting. Chargers (or underplates) are a smart alternative to a placemat, bring grandeur to the tabletop and can also add colour or pattern. Choose a tone that complements the china and the cloth to bring the look together.

Invest in as many settings as you require (a standard service for six or eight is a good starting point) and think about which pieces you really need. Would you prefer individual cereal, soup and dessert bowls, or one dish that does it all? Will you get more use from capacious pasta bowls or streamlined dinner plates? If a matching set is a priority, check that your chosen china is a stock item so that broken pieces will be easily replaceable.

Today, there are many styles of dinnerware available, from rustic earthenware to modern melamine to delicate vintage china, and most of us end up with a combination of different pieces. As a rule of thumb, try to match the dinnerware to the occasion and to the food you are serving; decorative vintage plates are perfect for puddings or for teatime. Hunt around in antiques markets for those with fluted edges or floral patterns, and use a mixture of both to create an appealing old-fashioned tabletop.

The advantage of choosing a plain white set of china is that it will go with everything. But patterned services or even a completely mismatched collection can work just as well, and will make also your tabletop more personal and interesting.

If you want to add to your china cupboard, you'll be spoilt for choice. Homeware stores on the high street and the internet stock a vast array of modern designs, while antiques shops and auction houses are both good sources of inexpensive vintage pieces. What you end up with will depend largely on your taste and your budget, of course, but don't forget to consider the practicalities. Do you have storage space for that stack of chunky bamboo bowls, and will you mind handwashing those pretty retro plates?

To keep your china in mint condition, store it carefully and make sure that everyday dinnerware is easy to access. Shelves of varying depth are very useful, giving separate space for glasses, serving bowls and dinnerware.

Finally, if you don't want to handwash china, make sure any new pieces are dishwasher-safe before you buy.

Glassware

Pretty glasses can be the making of a dinner table, adding sparkle and height to an otherwise flat array of tableware. Today, there are many styles available, from utilitarian tumblers to dainty flutes and etched cocktail glasses and, while any drinking glass should, above all, be functional, it can also add a lovely decorative element to your tabletop.

It's a good idea to start off with a basic collection of glasses that includes a variety of shapes and sizes, giving you the flexibility to cater for several different occasions. While you might make do with a simple tumbler or wine glass for everyday meals, you may want a wider selection when you have friends for supper or serve both red and white wine for a special lunch or dinner. It's sensible to start off with a mixed collection of good-quality glasses that works for you; you can always supplement it with the odd vintage piece or junk-shop find at a later date. Decorative glassware adds an extra dimension to a tabletop, particularly if it highlights or continues a theme. Adding just a few pieces of ornate or unusual glassware to the table – a pretty antique jug, perhaps, a modern carafe or some jewel-coloured water glasses – brings an extra decorative element to any scheme.

Invest in a wide selection of drinkware – from vintage wine goblets to cute and colourful, hand-decorated tumblers – so that you can mix and match different shapes and styles on the tabletop to suit every occasion.

Drinking glasses can also be used as inspired 'dishes' for delicate puddings. A slender-stemmed cocktail glass or champagne coupe can be perfect for serving a sweet jelly or sharp lemon cream,

while little shot glasses are just the right size for a rich chocolate mousse. You might also want to use pieces of glassware to display flowers on the tabletop. A row of tiny tumblers filled with grasses and blossoms can make a lovely focal point, and even a single perfect bloom popped in a liqueur glass will bring a table to life.

While it is tempting to choose pieces on the basis of looks alone, it's worth remembering that the design of a glass can affect the taste of what you are drinking. Sipping water from a chunky ceramic mug, for example, just doesn't feel right, while a beer glass will do nothing to enhance the flavours of an expensive wine. Try to provide suitable glasses for whatever drinks you are serving and buy the best you can afford. Thin clear glass or crystal is considered top of the range.

One last thing to think about before you splash out on that set of vintage 1930s cocktail glasses is the washing-up. Most antique glassware should not be washed in the dishwasher and even good modern pieces can go cloudy over time or are easily broken. Do remember that expensive glassware should be washed by hand and the dishwasher reserved for everyday items that are easily and cheaply replaced.

Cutlery

Given that the knife, fork and spoon are simply tools for eating, it is remarkable quite how many different designs you can find today. Cutlery comes in all kinds of materials – silver, stainless steel, plastic, wood, bamboo – and a wide variety of styles, from the very basic to the very decorative.

Households used to own a vast array of different pieces, but modern canteens are less lavish: a set of knives, forks, dessert spoons and teaspoons is standard. A simple collection such as this should be enough for every day, but it can be useful to add some extras over time. Steak knives, for example, are not part of a basic canteen, but will be handy if you eat a lot of red meat; soup spoons are very useful, and dessert forks, though rarely included, are perfect for tea parties.

While good-quality modern cutlery tends to be expensive, old sets can be incredibly cheap. If you need to supplement your existing collection, scour junk shops, eBay, auction houses and street markets and you might unearth some treasures: enamel-handled teaspoons, perhaps, or pretty bone butter knives. Vintage cutlery may not be as practical as its modern counterparts, but it will bring instant charm and character to your table. Make sure your vintage cutlery is dry before you store it to prevent tarnishing. Bone-handled pieces or silver plate should not go in the dishwasher so will have to be washed by hand.

If you want to invest in new cutlery, try it out before you buy. Each piece should feel well-balanced and the handle should sit comfortably in your hand. For a quirky contemporary look, seek out vintage designs made from modern materials. A plastic set will add interest, colour and texture to a tabletop. Inexpensive, tactile and eco-friendly, bamboo cutlery is easy to find and perfect for an informal or outdoor lunch.

How to set a table

A table setting is there to be used, so don't fret too much about etiquette or conventions. The intention is simply to provide the diner with the right tools in the right place for whatever dishes are on the menu. Here are a a few classic formations – start with a well-laid table and add a few well-chosen decorative elements and you are ready for almost any style of event.

International informal

This basic table setting will work for any informal Western meal and can be adapted depending on the food being served. Cutlery is positioned in the most convenient place for the diner: dinner fork to the left of the dinner plate; knives and soup spoons to the right and dessert forks and spoons above the plate, with handles facing the hand that will be using them. The glasses are positioned at the top right, with the largest glass (generally the red wine glass) set at the back for neatness.

1 Napkin in a simple fold
2 Dinner fork
3 Dinner plate
4 Dinner knife
5 Soup spoon
6 Dessert spoon
7 Dessert fork
8 White wine glass
9 Red wine glass
10 Water glass

1 Napkin in a simple fold
2 Butter plate
3 Dinner fork
4 Dessert fork
5 Dinner plate
6 Dessert spoon
7 Dinner knife
8 Soup spoon
9 White wine glass
10 Red wine glass
11 Water glass

British formal

For a dinner party, you may want to use a more formal table setting involving a wider selection of tableware. In this case, all the cutlery for the meal can be placed either side of the dinner plate and should be laid from the outside in so that the first-course cutlery is outermost (and thus most accessible) and the dessert spoon and fork innermost. A side plate for bread can be set to the left, and if you want to supply a butter knife, this can be laid across the plate in line with the edge of the table.

1 Napkin in a simple fold
2 Butter plate
3 Bread knife
4 Dessert spoon
5 Pastry fork
6 Saucer
7 Teacup
8 Teaspoon

English afternoon tea

If you are serving a formal sit-down tea, make sure you provide appropriate utensils for whatever food you are offering. You may need a butter knife, a pastry fork and even a spoon for a particularly creamy cake. These implements should all be set to the right of the plate, with the napkin placed on the left (or on top of the plate if you prefer). For a proper afternoon tea, it's imperative to use your very best teacups and saucers; mugs just won't give you the same sense of occasion.

American formal

Very similar to the British formal style, the American setting also places cutlery for each course either side of the dinner plate, working from the outside in. Here, the first course is a fish dish, so the outermost items are a fish knife and fork. Cutlery for the main course and pudding then follow. Americans tend to place bread or salad plates to the top left of the setting rather than at the side. Glasses are set in the standard triangular formation.

1 Napkin in a simple fold
2 Fish fork
3 Dinner fork
4 Pudding fork
5 Dinner plate
6 Dessert spoon
7 Dinner knife
8 Fish knife
9 White wine glass
10 Red wine glass
11 Water glass
12 Butter plate

French formal

Unlike the British and Americans, the French place their cutlery face down on the table and use a tablespoon for soup instead of a rounded soup spoon. Side plates and butter knives are not required, as bread is placed directly on the table and butter is not generally served. Cutlery is laid out in a standard Western style, but a knife rest is sometimes used so that the dinner knife can be laid back on the table and reused for the cheese course, which in France is served before the dessert.

1 Napkin in a simple fold
2 Dinner fork
3 Pudding fork
4 Dinner plate
5 Dessert spoon
6 Dinner knife
7 Soup spoon
8 White wine glass
9 Red wine glass
10 Water glass

1 Dinner plate
2 Chopsticks
3 Chopstick stand
4 Sauce dish
5 Teacup
6 Soup bowl
7 Soup spoon
8 Saucer

Chinese informal

A standard Western dinner plate, side plate and bowl can just as easily form part of a Chinese table setting, but a few extra accessories will be required to finish it off. You'll need a handleless teacup for jasmine or green tea; a Chinese soup spoon; a little dish for dipping sauces; chopsticks and a chopstick stand. You may also need an extra rice bowl if you are serving both soup and rice, but this can be brought to the table as needed. And conventional cutlery should be made available for guests who are inexperienced with chopsticks.

1 Rice bowl
2 Chopsticks
3 Chopstick stand
4 Soup bowl
5 Pickle dish
6 Teacup
7 Dinner plate

Japanese informal

Much like the Chinese setting, the Japanese table requires a number of bowls, dishes and plates for serving all the elements of a Japanese meal. Rice, noodles and soups are served in a bowl; sushi and sashimi, fried and grilled dishes are served on an open plate. Small dishes are needed for sauces and pickles, and a handleless teacup for miso soup. A small jug can also be used for soy sauce so that guests can help themselves. Chopsticks should be positioned right at the front of the setting with the ends pointing towards the left.

Flowers and focal point

The simplest and quickest way to bring a table to life is with flowers. Not only do they add colour and interest to a scheme, but they will also give a special touch to any occasion and need not cost a great deal of money.

For tabletop flowers, large structured bouquets aren't necessary. Something simple and subtle works best, even for a smart dinner. Single stems (or even just individual flowerheads) placed in glasses along the centre of the table are far more modern than a stiff, formal display.

If you don't have time to dash to the florist, raid the garden or windowbox for suitable specimens. A jug of simple peonies, poppies or even cow parsley is perfect for an informal meal. Choose flowers that complement your tableware, or use them as the starting point for the table's decorative scheme. The soft pink of an orchid can be picked up in a napkin tie or a tablemat, for example, while white anemones or hellebores could form the focal point of an all-white winter lunch table.

If you want to place flowers in the middle of the table, make sure the arrangement is not too tall; your guests should be able to see over it easily in order to chat. If you have created a large and dramatic display, it's best to position it at the end of the table or move it to one side at the start of the meal. Avoid strongly scented flowers, as they can put guests off the food. Ideally, stick to unscented blooms or remove strongly perfumed displays from the table before you eat.

How you present flowers is up to you, but generally, the more creative you are, the more impact the arrangement will have. To make a change from conventional vases, dream up alternative ways of displaying flowers. A variety of differently sized glass containers can be filled to the brim with flowers to make a striking modern arrangement. Recycled food packaging, such as glass kilner jars, vintage tin caddies or brightly coloured plastic containers, make quirky and eye-catching flower holders.

Instead of the usual bunch of flowers in a vase, experiment with single blooms in tumblers or eggcups. Also, a large bowl or a vintage glass cake stand can make a lovely focal point for a teatime tabletop. Hunt in flea-markets and second-hand stores for old-fashioned designs, or buy a reproduction piece. You could even scatter petals across the tabletop. Flowers should be an eye-catching focal point, so play around with different effects and see what works best.

If you're entertaining on the spur of the moment and don't have any flowers to hand, there are countless other ways to create an effective display. A large platter of seasonal fruit is another good option. An unusual focal point will bring charm and personality to a table, but don't be tempted to overdo it. The trick is to make sure that all the elements of the tabletop work together in harmony rather than one detail grabbing all the attention.

Remember too that a focal point needn't be confined to the middle of the tabletop. For a splash of colour overhead, hang vivid paper lanterns above the table. Perfect for an Eastern-style feast.

Candles and lighting

Getting the lighting right is crucial when it comes to creating a welcoming, hospitable atmosphere to eat by, and achieving the elusive 'not-too-bright-yet-not-too-dim' light level usually demands a spot of experimentation. There's no magic formula, as the level of light you will require varies depending on the season, the time of day and the brightness of your room, so building a flexible lighting system is key.

A good starting point is to get both overhead lights and table or floor lamps fitted with a dimmer switch so that you can easily and swiftly tweak the lighting levels. Then simply add candlelight. This most ancient of light sources not only casts a magical glow but brings warmth and atmosphere to any occasion – and you can't have too much of it.

Candles come in hundreds of different colours, shapes and sizes, so it will be easy to find something to suit your colour scheme, whether it's all green for Christmas lunch or all black for a dramatic monochrome setting. While plain white candles work with any tabletop scheme, colourful ones will add an extra decorative dimension. Choose one tone for a strong visual impact, or for a kitsch modern table, mix up a variety of bright colours in a candelabra or in separate candlesticks placed down the middle of the table – great for a quirky contemporary look.

Tiny tealights can be popped into any container to make a sparkly focal point. Although they are the cheapest and humblest candles of them all, they can

be the most effective when used en masse. Displayed in pretty glasses and lined up in a row, or set in little glass holders and scattered randomly around the cloth, they will bring instant glitz to any tabletop. Try to find something that matches your tableware; ceramic pots work perfectly with rustic earthenware or painted Moroccan tea-glasses make pretty containers.

Candles can be displayed in all manner of ways, so choose something that works with the occasion: an elegant candelabra for a formal dinner, for example, or a simple tealight popped in a glass jar for an evening barbecue. Use a cluster of candles of different heights, pieces of glittering glassware or a dramatic candelabra. Hunt around in flea markets and second-hand stores for lovely old mercury glass candlesticks or simply use whatever you have to hand.

Other decorative details

Often it's the finishing touches that you add to a tabletop that make it your own. While smart china, sleek silverware and glittering glassware will make any table look elegant, it's the last-minute flourishes and personal details that put an individual stamp on it.

A good starting point is a look through your cupboards for any hand-me-down bits and pieces: vintage napkin rings, perhaps, or the silver serving spoons that your granny gave you. Flea-markets or museum stores can yield one-off treasures: antique salt and pepper pots, perhaps, or a beautiful glass salad bowl. There's no formula for successful finishing touches; it's just about adding a few things you love to make the tabletop special.

As well as being practical, vintage carafes or decanters can add a decorative dimension to a tabletop and can often be found at bargain prices in flea markets or at auction.

Find interesting ways to serve seasonings. Vintage metal egg poachers are perfect for coarse sea salt and cracked black pepper; more individual pieces, such as little silver birds (right), will add a personal touch.

The napkin ring is the perfect dress-up accessory on the tabletop and can add all sorts of sparkle and glamour to a table setting. Whether they are in the shape of a crystal flower, in antique polished silver or just a length of vivid ribbon or brocade, napkin rings bring a welcome decorative element and can jazz up even the plainest white china and table linen.

The best way to personalize a place setting is to give it a name. Handwrite guests' names on cards, tags or even slate tiles, and pop them in the middle of each plate. If you don't want to clutter your tabletop with bits and pieces, there are more subtle ways to personalize the table. Write guests' names on pretty cards or chalk them on slate placemats. Using unusual materials for the tablecloth, the mats and the coasters (be it embroidered felt or vintage wallpaper) will add a quirky, unexpected edge to the tabletop. Be inventive and have fun.

Don't reserve your decorative efforts solely for the tabletop – think about how to dress up the rest of the room, too. Pretty garlands are a good way to echo the elements of a table scheme and easy to assemble. Rose petals strung onto thin wire (fishing line would be a good alternative) and hung in a swag at the window make a fabulous finishing touch.

brunch dishes

Bircher muesli

125 g rolled oats

75 g sultanas

175 ml pure apple juice

freshly squeezed juice of
1 lemon

100 g natural yoghurt

1 apple, cored, peeled
and roughly grated

25 g flaked almonds

mixed summer berries,
to serve

clear honey, to serve

Serves 4–6

Put the oats and sultanas in
a large dish. Pour over the
apple and lemon juices. Cover
with a tea towel and leave to
soak overnight. Alternatively
combine everything in an
airtight container and put
in the fridge.

The next morning when
you're ready for brunch,
stir the yoghurt, apple and
almonds into the soaked
muesli. Divide between
serving bowls, scatter some
berries over the top and finish
with a drizzle of honey.

*This is a good alternative to porridge for
summer. It has the type of texture you either
love or hate – there is something comforting
about its soggy sweetness. It will keep for
2–3 days in the fridge, but if you plan to
store it for that long, leave the apple out so
it doesn't brown.*

Granola, nectarine and ricotta parfait

150 g natural
sheep's yoghurt

250 g ricotta

300 g Nutty Honey
Granola (page 32)

4 nectarines, stoned
and sliced

100 g raspberries

4 tablespoons clear
honey, plus extra to
drizzle

Serves 4

These little pots of deliciousness are perfect to offer guests at a brunch party. Layer the ricotta, fruit and granola in glasses for an attractive look. You can vary the fruit depending on the season, but if you use hard fruits, such as apples or pears, poach them in some sugar syrup first until they are as soft as a ripe nectarine.

Put the yoghurt and ricotta in a bowl and beat together until combined. Divide half the granola between 4 glasses, then put some nectarine slices and raspberries on top of that. Top with some of the yoghurt mixture and honey. Top with the remaining granola, followed by more nectarines and raspberries, saving a few for the top, and another spoonful or two of the yoghurt mixture. Arrange the remaining fruit on top, drizzle with more honey and serve immediately.

Nutty honey granola

Mmmm, crunchy honeyed granola. This version is very sweet and crunchy and quite rich so a little goes a long way. Try it scattered over yoghurt rather than the other way round. The trick is to get it to brown evenly, so you need the mixture to be spread out in one layer and to turn it during roasting. Don't let it become too dark or it will taste bitter. If in doubt, take it out of the oven and leave it to cool a little, then taste it. You can always put it back in for longer.

125 g pure maple syrup

125 g clear honey

4 tablespoons sunflower oil

250 g rolled oats

75 g shelled almonds, roughly chopped

75 g shelled Brazil nuts, roughly chopped

50 g pumpkin seeds

½ teaspoon sea salt

100 g sultanas

2 baking trays, lined with baking parchment

Serves 10–12

Preheat the oven to 140°C (275°F) Gas 1.

Put the maple syrup, honey and oil in a small saucepan and set over low heat to warm though. Put the oats, nuts, seeds and salt in a large mixing bowl and stir well. Pour over the warmed syrup and mix thoroughly with a wooden spoon. All the oats must be moistened.

Spread the granola over the prepared baking trays, making sure it is no deeper than 1 cm, and bake in the preheated oven for 20 minutes.

Remove the trays from the oven and stir the toasted, golden granola from the edges to the centre, then smooth out again. Return to the oven for a further 15–20 minutes, until lightly golden. Don't expect it to become crunchy – the mixture will remain soft until it cools.

Remove from the oven and leave to cool for 10 minutes before stirring in the sultanas. Leave to cool completely, then break into pieces. Store in an airtight container and eat within 1 month.

Blueberry pancakes

Perfect blueberry pancakes should be light and fluffy, with a good rise on them. The secret is to use some water – an all-milk batter makes the pancakes heavier. And remember to serve them with plenty of maple syrup.

125 g self-raising flour

1 teaspoon baking powder

2 tablespoons caster sugar

¼ teaspoon salt

1 egg

100 ml whole milk

50 g butter, melted

150 g blueberries,
plus extra to serve

maple syrup, to serve

Serves 4

Preheat the oven to 130°C (250°F) Gas ½.

Sift the flour and baking powder into a large mixing bowl and stir in the sugar and salt. Put the egg, milk and 75 ml water in a jug and beat to combine.

Stir half the butter into the wet ingredients in the jug. Mix the wet ingredients with the dry ingredients until no lumps of flour remain.

Wipe a heavy-based frying pan with a scrunched-up piece of kitchen paper dipped in the remaining melted butter. Heat up, then drop in 4 tablespoons of the batter. Cook for 1–2 minutes on the first side, then scatter over a few of the blueberries and flip the pancake over. Cook for 2 minutes, until golden and cooked through. Keep warm in the oven while you make the rest.

Serve with more blueberries and maple syrup for pouring.

Eggs benedict

This dish is all about timing. Get everything ready before you cook the eggs and you won't have to rush. Hollandaise sauce made in a blender is easy – just add the butter very slowly and you should hear the sauce turning thick and slushy.

4 large eggs

4 wholemeal English muffins, halved horizontally

8 slices of thin-cut ham

freshly ground black pepper

Hollandaise sauce

2 tablespoons white wine vinegar

1 shallot, roughly chopped

½ teaspoon whole black peppercorns

2 large egg yolks

120 g unsalted butter

Serves 4

Preheat the grill.

To make the hollandaise sauce put the vinegar, shallot and peppercorns in a saucepan and add 2 tablespoons cold water. Simmer over low heat for a few minutes until you have 1 tablespoon liquid remaining. Strain into a blender (or in a bowl if you are going to use an electric handheld mixer) with the egg yolks and set aside. Melt the butter in the same saucepan.

Fill a large, deep frying pan with water and bring to a low simmer. Crack the eggs around the edge of the pan so they don't touch and poach for exactly 3 minutes.

Put the muffins (cut side up) and ham on a baking tray and grill for 2–3 minutes.

To finish the sauce, blend the eggs and vinegar until frothy. With the motor still running, add the melted butter in a very slow trickle until the sauce is thick. You should take about a minute to add all the butter. Any quicker and it will not emulsify and you'll be left with runny eggs.

Drape a slice of ham on top of each muffin half. Scoop out each poached egg and add to the stack. Pour over the hollandaise sauce and grind over some black pepper.

Scrambled eggs with smoked trout and shiso

Scrambled eggs need to be cooked with patience to become creamy. If they are cooked properly, you will not have to resort to adding cream, which just hides an underlying bad scramble. Smoked trout goes exceedingly well with scrambled eggs and the pretty purple leaves of shiso cress decorate it and add a spicy kick.

10 large eggs

4 tablespoons whole milk

50 g butter

4 slices of white bread

280 g hot smoked trout, flaked

a handful of shiso cress

a pinch of Japanese chilli pepper or chilli powder

sea salt and freshly ground black pepper

Serves 4

Break the eggs into a mixing bowl and beat together with the milk and some salt and pepper.

Heat half the butter in a heavy-based saucepan set over low heat until the bubbling subsides. Pour in the eggs and heat through, stirring occasionally, for 4–5 minutes, until they start to feel like they are in danger of catching on the base of the pan. Reduce the heat to its lowest setting and stir constantly for 3–5 minutes to make sure the eggs

are not over-heating on the bottom of the pan.

Meanwhile, toast the bread and spread with the remaining butter.

Take the eggs off the heat while they still look a little runny, add the trout, give them a final few stirs and divide between the pieces of toast. Scatter the shiso and a little chilli pepper over the top and serve immediately.

Garlic mushrooms and goats' cheese on sourdough toast

8 field mushrooms

3 garlic cloves, crushed

3 tablespoons olive oil

25 g pine nuts

2 tablespoons balsamic
vinegar

4 slices of sourdough bread

150 g fresh goats' cheese

fresh tarragon, to serve

sea salt and freshly ground
black pepper

Serves 4

Garlicky mushrooms are great for breakfast, but try them on a layer of soft, creamy goats' cheese and you will be in utter heaven. The kind of cheese you are looking for is a soft fresh cheese, not aged, so it will not have a rind. You could also use ricotta if you like. Seek out a good, sturdy rustic bread such as sourdough for this dish to prevent the underneath from going soggy.

Preheat the oven to 200°C (400°F) Gas 6.

Put the mushrooms, garlic and oil in a roasting tray. Toss well and season. Roast in the preheated oven for 15 minutes, until tender. Stir in the pine nuts and balsamic vinegar halfway through the roasting time.

Just before the mushrooms are ready, toast the slices of sourdough bread and spread with the goats' cheese. Arrange the mushrooms on top, scatter with the tarragon, add more seasoning if necessary and serve immediately.

Reubens with beef, sauerkraut and emmenthal

This is a classic American sandwich which contains corned beef (or salt beef), tangy dressing, sauerkraut and melted Swiss cheese. It makes a delicious and substantial brunch dish, perfect for entertaining.

4 tablespoons mayonnaise

3 spring onions, sliced

2 gherkins, chopped

¼ teaspoon hot horseradish sauce

a dash of Worcestershire sauce

a pinch of caster sugar

8 slices of rye bread

300 g corned or salt beef, sliced

200 g sauerkraut, drained

100 g Emmenthal, sliced

Serves 4

Put the mayonnaise, spring onions, gherkins, horseradish sauce, Worcestershire sauce and sugar in a bowl, mix well and set aside.

Preheat the grill. Grill the bread for about 1–2 minutes on one side, until golden. Remove from under the grill and spread some dressing over the untoasted side of half the slices. Lay the Emmenthal on the rest and return to the grill for 2–3 minutes to melt the cheese.

Meanwhile, put the corned beef, then some sauerkraut over the dressing-covered bread slices. Once the cheese has melted, make up the sandwiches and serve immediately, while they are still hot.

Smoked salmon kedgeree

3 large eggs

250 g undyed skinless, smoked haddock or cod fillet

250 g lightly smoked skinless, salmon fillet or ordinary salmon fillet

3 tablespoons sunflower oil

1 onion, finely chopped

2–3 teaspoons mild curry powder

300 g basmati rice

175 g cooked shelled prawns

40 g butter, softened

2–3 tablespoons freshly squeezed lemon juice

3 heaped tablespoons chopped coriander leaves, plus a few whole leaves to garnish

sea salt and freshly ground black pepper

Serves 6

Kedgeree is an Anglo-Indian dish that stems from the days of the Raj. This party version is based on a relatively new product – lightly smoked salmon, which gives it a particularly luxurious flavour. If you can't find it, use organic salmon and add a little bit of smoked salmon at the end when you add the prawns.

Bring a small saucepan of water to the boil. Lower the eggs carefully into the water and boil for 10–12 minutes. Drain off the water, pour cold running water over the eggs, then leave to cool in cold water.

Put the smoked haddock and salmon in a large saucepan and pour over just enough cold water to cover. Bring gradually to the boil, then once the water is bubbling, take the pan off the heat and cover it with a lid or a piece of kitchen foil. Leave for 5 minutes, then remove the fish fillets. Pour the cooking water into a jug up to the 600 ml mark and set aside.

Heat the oil in another heavy-duty saucepan or a flameproof casserole and fry the onion over moderate heat for about 6–7 minutes, until starting to turn dark brown at the edges. Sprinkle in the curry powder to taste. Add the rice, stir again and pour in the reserved water you used for cooking the fish. Bring to the boil then turn the heat right down and cover the pan with a lid. Cook for about 15–20 minutes until all the liquid has been absorbed.

Meanwhile, shell and quarter the boiled eggs. Set aside 6 quarters and roughly chop the rest. Flake the fish, being very careful to remove any remaining bones. Once the rice is cooked, fork it through and tip in the cooked fish, prawns and chopped eggs, cover the pan and leave for 5 minutes over very low heat. Turn off the heat, add the butter, fork through. Season to taste with the lemon juice and a little salt and pepper if you think it needs it and fork through the chopped coriander. Serve on a warmed platter garnished with the quartered eggs and the remaining coriander leaves.

You can keep the kedgeree warm in a covered pan for about 15–20 minutes before serving or transfer it to a very low oven for 30–40 minutes, but no longer as it will begin to dry out.

Huevos rancheros

3 tablespoons vegetable oil

1 fresh green chilli, chopped

2 garlic cloves, crushed

500 g tomatoes, cut into thin wedges

400-g tin pinto or cannellini beans, drained and rinsed

50 g Cheddar, grated

freshly squeezed juice of 1 lime, plus extra lime wedges to serve

a handful of fresh coriander leaves, chopped

4 eggs

4 corn tortillas

sea salt and freshly ground black pepper

lime wedges, for squeezing

guacamole and/or soured cream, to serve (optional)

Serves 4

There are numerous versions of these 'ranch eggs'. This recipe combines spicy fresh tomato salsa with mashed, cheesy beans. You can buy tins of prepared refried beans but it is just as easy to mash your own. If you want to serve it with a spoonful of guacamole or soured cream, that's a great idea.

Heat 1 tablespoon of the oil in a large frying pan set over medium heat, then add the chilli, half the garlic and a pinch of salt and fry for 1–2 minutes, until softened. Add the tomatoes and cook gently for about 20 minutes.

Heat the remaining oil in a small saucepan, add the remaining garlic and heat through for 20 seconds, until just browning. Add the beans, then using a potato masher, coarsely mash them and stir in the Cheddar. Season to taste.

Stir the lime juice and coriander into the tomato sauce. Make 4 holes in the sauce and crack an egg into each one. Cook for 3 minutes until just set. Cover with a lid for the last 30 seconds just to firm up the whites.

Meanwhile, heat another frying pan over medium heat. Dry fry the tortillas for 1 minute on each side, until golden and hot.

Transfer to 4 serving plates and spread the mashed beans over the tortillas. Top with tomato salsa and the eggs. Serve with lime wedges for squeezing and dollops of guacamole and/or soured cream if you like.

Potato and rosemary pancakes with bacon and honey

500 g potatoes, peeled

1 tablespoon finely chopped fresh rosemary needles

150 g plain flour

½ teaspoon bicarbonate of soda

275 ml buttermilk

12 rashers of streaky bacon

25 g butter

sea salt and freshly ground black pepper

clear honey or pure maple syrup, to serve

Serves 4

These pancakes are based on the Irish potato dish called boxty, in which some of the potatoes are cooked and mashed, and the others are grated to give the pancakes a bit of texture on top of the fluffiness. They were obviously once seen as a sign of domesticity, as they prompted the saying: 'Boxty on the griddle, boxty in the pan, if you can't make boxty, you'll never get a man'.

Put 300 g of the potatoes in a saucepan of cold, salted water and bring to the boil. Cook for 20–25 minutes, until soft. Drain and mash, then season and add the rosemary. Leave to cool.

Meanwhile, peel and grate the remaining potatoes and leave them raw. Put both sets of potato in a mixing bowl and beat in the flour and bicarbonate of soda, then the buttermilk.

Preheat the grill.

Grill the bacon until well done (there's no need to turn it over while it's being grilled). Leave to cool for 4–5 minutes, until crisp. Turn off the grill and keep the bacon warm in a low oven while you continue cooking.

Heat half the butter in a frying pan set over low/medium heat and wait for it to sizzle. Drop 2–3 ladlefuls of the batter into the pan, spaced apart, and spread out with a spatula. They need about 3 minutes on the first side, then a little less on the other side. Keep warm with the bacon in the oven while you cook the rest.

Serve 2–3 pancakes per person, with a few rashers of bacon and some honey or maple syrup to drizzle over the top.

Cheesy polenta with sausages and red onions

12 pork sausages

2 red onions, peeled and cut into slim wedges

a handful of fresh sage leaves

6 tablespoons olive oil

150 g instant polenta

1 tablespoon chopped fresh thyme leaves

50 g Parmesan, grated

200 g feta, crumbled

sea salt and freshly ground black pepper

a 20-cm square baking tin, greased

Serves 4

If you are not yet sold on polenta, do try this method of preparation because it has converted many a person. The secret is that it needs to be seasoned well and enriched with lots of cheese, as well as being fried over high heat until golden so that you get the crunchy exterior and the soft creaminess inside.

Preheat the oven to 190°C (375°F) Gas 5.

Put the sausages and onions in a roasting tray. Scatter the sage over the top and drizzle with 2 tablespoons of the oil, then toss everything together. Roast in the preheated oven for about 30–35 minutes, until golden and cooked through.

Bring 650 ml water to the boil with a pinch of salt and 1 tablespoon of the oil. Remove from the heat and pour in the polenta. Mix it with a wooden spoon and lots of elbow grease. Return to low heat for about 2–3 minutes, stirring constantly. Remove from the heat, beat in the thyme and cheeses and season generously. Spoon into the prepared baking tin and smooth out the surface. Leave to cool and set.

Tip the polenta onto a board and quarter, then cut each quarter in half to make triangles. Heat a frying pan over high heat and add the remaining oil. Add as many polenta triangles as you can and fry for 2–3 minutes on each side, until crisp and golden. Arrange the fried polenta on serving plates and spoon the sausage mixture over the top.

Sweet potato pancakes with hot smoked trout and chilli-lime butter

a 250-g sweet potato, peeled

3 tablespoons sunflower oil, plus extra for frying

225 ml whole milk

1 egg

130 g plain flour

2 teaspoons baking powder

a pinch of cayenne pepper

2 teaspoons fish sauce

225 g hot smoked trout

fresh coriander, to garnish

Chilli-lime butter

2 spring onions, sliced

1 fresh red chilli, shredded

1 teaspoon finely grated fresh ginger

1 teaspoon demerara sugar

2 teaspoons fish sauce

freshly squeezed juice of 2 limes

75 g unsalted butter

Serves 4

This Thai-inspired recipe makes an unusual and delicious brunch dish. Using fish sauce instead of salt adds an Asian seasoning and the chilli-lime butter soaks into the moist potato pancakes and really brings out their sweetness. All the flavours work beautifully together and it makes a change from the more usual maple syrup and pancake combination.

Preheat the oven to low.

Halve the sweet potato and put it in a saucepan of boiling water. Simmer for about 25 minutes until really soft. Test with a knife to check it is cooked through.

Drain the potato and mash with the oil. Stir in the milk and leave the mixture to cool before beating in the egg. Sift in the flour, baking powder and cayenne pepper, and season with the fish sauce instead of salt. Set aside.

To make the chilli-lime butter, mix together the spring onions, chilli, ginger, sugar, fish sauce and lime juice to make a dressing and set aside.

Heat a frying pan or flat griddle pan over medium heat. Grease the pan with a scrunched up piece of kitchen paper dipped in oil. Drop in 2 tablespoons of the potato batter and cook for about 2 minutes on the first side, until bubbles appear and the edges are dry. Flip over and cook on the other side for a further 2 minutes. Keep warm in the oven while you cook the rest.

To finish the chilli-lime butter, melt the butter in a small saucepan and stir in the dressing. Arrange the pancakes on serving plates, top with trout and coriander, and pour over the warm chilli-lime butter. Serve immediately.

Hot smoked salmon hash with dill crème fraîche

500 g new potatoes, halved

4 tablespoons olive oil

2 onions, sliced

150 g streaky bacon, chopped

15 g butter

2 teaspoons capers

200 g hot smoked salmon

150 g crème fraîche

freshly squeezed juice and grated zest of 1 lime

1 tablespoon chopped fresh dill

sea salt and freshly ground black pepper

Serves 4

Set a large saucepan of water over medium heat and bring to the boil. Add a pinch of salt and the potatoes. Reduce the heat and leave to simmer for 12–15 minutes, until the potatoes are tender.

Meanwhile, put half the oil, the onions and bacon in a frying pan. Cover with a lid and cook over low heat for 8–10 minutes, stirring occasionally, until softening. Remove the lid, turn up the heat slightly and cook for about 3–4 minutes until slightly golden. Tip onto a plate and set aside.

Drain the potatoes and add the butter and remaining oil to the frying pan you just used for the onion mixture. Add the potatoes and cook over high heat for 5–6 minutes, until browning on all sides. Stir in the onion mixture, capers and salmon (breaking it into pieces before adding) and cook for 3–4 minutes, until everything is sizzling and hot, then season to taste.

Mix together the crème fraîche, lime zest and enough juice to give it flavour, but not so much that it becomes runny. Stir in the dill and season. Serve the hash with the crème fraîche on the side.

Unlike the regular smoked salmon we know so well, hot smoked salmon looks cooked and flakes into beautiful chunks. Mixing it with streaky bacon works really well as they share the same smokiness. A dollop of crème fraîche infused with lime and dill and served on the side adds freshness.

Steak and fried egg baps with mustard butter

A well-cooked steak with a rosy interior and charred exterior truly is a wonderful thing. Here it is adorned with a butter spiked with the piquant flavour of mustard and tarragon. When the steak is ready, it is sandwiched in a soft white bap slathered in a delicious mustard butter, which will melt with the steak's residual heat. Along with a fried egg cooked so it is still just runny inside, this is one sandwich that you need to eat fast before the egg and butter have time to trickle down your chin.

100 g butter, softened

2 teaspoons wholegrain mustard

½ teaspoon English mustard powder

1 tablespoon chopped fresh tarragon leaves

1 teaspoon Gentleman's relish or anchovy paste (optional)

2 white baps, halved horizontally

2 x 250-g rib-eye or sirloin steaks, roughly 1.5 cm thick

3 tablespoons olive oil

2 large eggs

sea salt and freshly ground black pepper

Serves 2

Put the butter in a mixing bowl and beat it with a spoon until soft. Add the wholegrain mustard, mustard powder, tarragon and relish, if using. Season to taste, taking care not to over-season as the relish will already be salty. Beat everything together and use to butter the insides of the baps.

Heat a ridged griddle pan over high heat until very hot. Brush the steaks with 1 tablespoon of the oil and season. Using tongs, lay the steaks on the griddle and press down. Leave them to cook for 2–4 minutes on each side. Press the centre of the steak to determine how well cooked it is.

A light yield means it is medium, while anything soft is still rare. Transfer the steaks to a board and cut off any large pieces of fat. Leave to rest for 2–3 minutes while you cook the eggs.

Add the remaining oil to a frying pan and heat over high heat. Crack in the eggs and turn the heat to low. Cook for 2 minutes, then flip over for 30 seconds to cook the other side, but leave the yolk with a bit of ooze. Place a fried egg in each buttered bap and finish off with a steak. Serve immediately, with plenty of napkins!

Bagels with smoked salmon and wasabi crème fraîche

A classic American brunch dish is given a modern twist here with the addition of fiery Japanese wasabi paste. These bagels are great for serving to a crowd, as they are quick and easy to prepare.

4 plain bagels

200 g crème fraîche

2–3 teaspoons wasabi paste

freshly ground black pepper

250 g smoked salmon

to serve

snipped chives

lemon wedges

Serves 4

Cut the bagels in half and toast lightly on both sides. Put the crème fraîche and wasabi paste in a small bowl and beat until evenly mixed. Add black pepper to taste, but not too much as the wasabi is already hot.

Spread 4 bagel halves with the wasabi mixture. Top with the smoked salmon and chives then add the remaining bagel halves. Serve with lemon wedges for squeezing.

Exploding berry crumble muffins

These look just like the muffins sold in coffee shops which seem to have exploded out of their cases with their generous proportions. There is no secret trick to this – just fill the muffin cases right up to the top!

375 g plain flour

3 teaspoons baking powder

1 teaspoon bicarbonate of soda

150 g golden caster sugar

½ teaspoon sea salt

2 eggs, beaten

115 g unsalted butter, melted

200 g soured cream

60 ml whole milk

180 g raspberries

Crumble topping

100 g plain flour

75 g butter, chilled and cubed

30 g golden caster sugar

30 g flaked almonds

a 12-hole muffin tin

Makes 12

Preheat the oven to 170°C (375°F) Gas 3. Line the muffin tin with paper cases and grease the surface of the tin where the muffins will rise and stick.

To make the crumble topping, put the flour and butter in a food processor and pulse briefly, just until the butter is blended. Tip out into a bowl and add the sugar and almonds, pressing the mixture together with your hands.

To make the muffins, sift the flour, baking powder, bicarbonate of soda, sugar and salt into a large mixing bowl. Put the eggs in a small jug, add the melted butter, soured cream and milk and whisk to combine. Pour the wet ingredients into the dry ingredients and scatter the raspberries on top. Using a large spoon, fold until the mixture is moistened. It needs to be lumpy and shouldn't be overworked otherwise the baked muffins will be tough. Spoon into the paper cases right to the top. For regular-sized (not exploding!) muffins you can spoon the cases two-thirds full – you will be able to make more of these with this amount of mixture. Finish by scattering over the topping.

Bake in the preheated oven for 25–28 minutes for large muffins, or 18–22 minutes for the smaller ones.

Leave to cool for 5 minutes in the tin before transferring to a wire rack.

Sugary jam doughnut muffins

75 g sunflower oil

150 g natural yoghurt

½ teaspoon vanilla extract

2 large eggs, beaten

275 g self-raising flour

½ teaspoon bicarbonate of soda

a pinch of salt

100 g caster sugar

75 g blueberry jam

Topping

25 g unsalted butter, melted

50 g caster sugar

a 6-hole muffin tin

Makes 6

This is a recipe for anyone who likes a warm sugary doughnut but dislikes the deep frying involved in making them. Of course the result is more cakey than bready but they are every bit as delicious, as they ooze jam and cover your lips with sugar crystals.

Preheat the oven to 190°C (375°F) Gas 5 and line the muffin tray with paper cases.

Put the oil, yoghurt, vanilla extract and eggs in a bowl and beat together.

In another, large bowl, mix together the flour, bicarbonate of soda, salt and sugar. Pour the wet ingredients into the dry ingredients and swiftly mix together, until just combined. It needs to be quite lumpy but you need to hassle any floury pockets until there are no more.

Drop 1 heaped tablespoon of the batter in each paper case. Make a dip in the mixture and spoon in a heaped teaspoon of the jam. Divide the remaining batter between the paper cases to cover the jam. Bake in the preheated oven for about 18–20 minutes, until well risen. Set aside, still in the tin, and leave to cool for 5 minutes before adding the sugary topping.

When the muffins have cooled for 5 minutes, brush their tops with the melted butter for the topping and roll in the sugar. Transfer to a wire rack to cool to room temperature.

nibbles and
sharing plates

Preheat the oven to 180°C (350°F) Gas 4.

Put all of the nuts in a large bowl. Add the cayenne pepper, paprika, thyme, salt and sugar and mix to combine. Stir in the olive oil. Tip the nuts out onto the prepared baking tray, spreading them out into a single layer.

Bake in the preheated oven for 10 minutes, stirring about halfway through the cooking time. Leave to cool completely before spooning into serving bowls. Perfect served with any of the drinks recipes given on page 168–178, these nuts will keep in an airtight container for 7–10 days.

Parmesan biscuits

This is a savoury biscuit made using an old catering trick – using clingfilm to roll the mixture into a log and then refrigerating it until needed. All you then have to do is slice the chilled dough and bake. Smoked paprika gives these a Spanish feel, making them great to serve with manchego cheese and quince paste.

125 g unsalted butter, cubed and softened

80 g mature Cheddar, grated

20 g Parmesan, finely grated

150 g plain flour

¼ teaspoon Spanish smoked paprika (pimentón dulce)

a baking tray, lined with baking parchment

Makes about 60

Combine the butter and both cheeses in a food processor. Add the flour and paprika and process until just combined and the mixture forms into lots of smaller balls of dough. Add about 1–2 tablespoons cold water and process until the dough roughly comes together.

Lay a sheet of clingfilm on a work surface and spoon half of the mixture down the centre to form a log, about 3 cm across. Firmly roll up. Repeat with the remaining dough to make 2 logs and refrigerate for about 1 hour, until firm. Alternatively, keep in the freezer until needed.

Preheat the oven to 180°C (350°F) Gas 4.

Finely slice the log and arrange the discs on the prepared baking tray. Bake in the preheated oven for 8–10 minutes and then transfer to a wire rack to cool and become crisp. These will keep in an airtight container for 2 days or you can freeze the uncooked dough for up to 1 month.

Spicy Cajun mixed nuts

Cashews, pecans and pistachios are used here, but feel free to choose your favourite nuts for this recipe. Buy the nuts in bulk and you will save heaps of cash. And besides, this is a recipe you will want to make more than once. It's a good nibble to offer with drinks if you are planning to serve a spicy meal later on.

160 g shelled cashews

160 g shelled pecans

140 g shelled pistachios

1 teaspoon cayenne pepper

1 teaspoon Spanish smoked paprika (pimentón dulce)

thyme

1 teaspoon fine sea salt

1 tablespoon soft brown sugar

1 tablespoon olive oil

a baking tray, lined with baking parchment

Serves 10–12

Mexican tostaditas and empanadas

Why not have a get-together with a Mexican flavour? You can serve these delicious little tostaditas and empanadas with ice cold margaritas for a fun way to start an evening.

Prawn and guacamole topping

Marinade

freshly squeezed juice of
½ a lime

1½ tablespoons olive oil

1 garlic clove, crushed

1 tablespoon finely chopped
fresh coriander

200 g cooked tiger prawns

200 g prepared or home-made
guacamole

large tortilla chips, to serve

*Makes sufficient to top
12–14 large tortilla chips*

Mix the ingredients for the marinade together and pour over
the prawns. Cover and marinate for at least 1 hour. Spoon the
guacamole onto the tortilla chips and top with a prawn. Serve
soon after making.

Crab, mango and basil topping

3 tablespoons mayonnaise

1 small fresh red chilli, deseeded
and finely chopped

2 spring onions, trimmed and
finely chopped

½ teaspoon grated fresh ginger

1–2 tablespoons freshly squeezed
lemon juice

175 g fresh white or white and
brown crab meat

75 g peeled and finely diced ripe
mango, plus mango shavings made
using a vegetable peeler or sharp
knife, to garnish

6 large basil leaves

sea salt and cayenne pepper

large tortilla chips, to serve

*Makes sufficient to top
12–14 large tortilla chips*

Mix the mayonnaise with the chilli, spring onions, ginger and
1 tablespoon of the lemon juice. Fold in the crab and mango.
Season to taste with salt, cayenne pepper and extra lemon juice.
Refrigerate. Just before serving, finely shred the basil leaves and
fold into the crab mixture. Spoon onto tortilla chips and top with
a mango shaving. Serve soon after making.

Pork and olive empanadas

*Empanadas are like mini Cornish pasties and make a
delicious and substantial hot bite to serve with drinks.*

3 tablespoons vegetable oil

450 g minced pork

1 onion, finely chopped

1 garlic clove, finely chopped

2 tablespoons tomato purée

½ teaspoon mixed spice

125 ml passata (sieved tomatoes)

1 tablespoon cider vinegar

10 pitted green olives, marinated
in garlic and herbs, chopped

2 tablespoons finely chopped
flat-leaf parsley

sea salt and freshly ground
black pepper

500 g ready-made puff pastry

1 large egg, beaten

2 large baking trays, greased

a 6-cm pastry cutter

Make 10–12

Heat 1 tablespoon of the olive oil in a large frying pan and brown
the mince. Transfer to a bowl with a slotted spoon and pour off
any remaining fat and meat juices. Add the remaining oil to
the pan and fry the chopped onion for about 6–7 minutes, until
beginning to brown. Add the garlic, fry for a few seconds, then
return the meat to the pan. Stir in the tomato purée and cook
for 1 minute, then add the mixed spice, passata and vinegar. Bring
to the boil and simmer for 10–15 minutes, until the excess liquid
has been absorbed.

Stir in the chopped olives and parsley, season to taste with salt
and pepper and set aside until cool (about 1 hour). Roll out the
pastry on a floured work surface. Stamp out rounds with the
pastry cutter and place a teaspoonful of the filling in the centre
of each one. Dampen the edges with water, fold over and press
the edges together. Repeat until you have used up all the pastry
and filling, re-rolling the pastry as necessary. At this point you
can refrigerate or freeze the empanadas until you need them.

Preheat the oven to 225°C (425°F) Gas 7. Cut a small slit in
the top of each empanada with a sharp knife and brush with
beaten egg. Put on the baking trays and bake in the preheated
oven for 8–10 minutes, until puffed up and golden (slightly longer
if cooking them from frozen). Serve warm with drinks.

Variation: For Cheese Empanadas, simply combine 230 g curd
cheese with 1 crushed garlic clove, 2 tablespoons finely chopped
shallot, 2 tablespoons finely chopped parsley and ¼ t
Spanish smoked paprika (pimentón). Take teaspoon
mixture and use to fill the empanadas, as described

Trio of root vegetable dips with spelt toasts

It's the vibrant colours of these dips that first grab your attention, quickly followed by the delicious flavours. Surprisingly, they are all made with humble and inexpensive root vegetables yet have rich creamy textures that contrast nicely with the nutty spelt toasts.

Roasted parsnip and garlic dip

25 g chilled unsalted butter, cubed

90 ml double cream

½ teaspoon sea salt

¼ teaspoon ground white pepper

500 g parsnips, peeled and sliced

1 garlic bulb, cut in half

Serves 6–8

Preheat the oven to 180°C (350°F) Gas 4. Lightly butter a small baking dish. Put the cream in a small bowl and stir in the salt and pepper.

Put the parsnips in the baking dish with the garlic. Pour the cream over the top, cover with kitchen foil and cook in the preheated oven for 45 minutes. Remove the garlic and let cool. When cool enough to handle, squeeze the soft, baked garlic directly into the bowl of a food processor or blender and discard the skin. Add the remaining ingredients and process until smooth. Transfer to a serving dish and cover until ready to serve.

Beetroot and caraway seed dip

3 medium beetroots, uncooked

1 tablespoon hot horseradish sauce

90 g soured cream

1 teaspoon caraway seeds

sea salt and ground white pepper

Serves 6–8

Put the beetroots in a large saucepan and cover with cold water. Bring to the boil and let boil for about 45–50 minutes, topping up the water from time to time as necessary. They are ready when a skewer goes through them with little resistance. Drain and leave to cool.

When cool enough to handle, peel and discard the skins. Roughly chop and put in a food processor or blender with the other ingredients and process until smooth. Transfer to a serving dish and cover until ready to serve.

Spiced carrot dip

250 ml good vegetable stock

4 medium carrots, chopped

2 tablespoons light olive oil

1 small red onion, chopped

2 garlic cloves, chopped

1 large fresh red chilli, chopped

1 teaspoon fenugreek seeds

1 teaspoon ground cumin

sea salt and ground white pepper

Serves 6–8

Put the stock in a saucepan and add the carrots, oil, onion and garlic. Bring to the boil, then reduce the heat to low and simmer for 15–20 minutes, until almost all the liquid has evaporated and the carrots are soft. Add the chilli, fenugreek and cumin and stir-fry for 2–3 minutes.

Transfer the mixture to a food processor or blender and whizz until blended but still with a rough texture. Season to taste, transfer to a serving dish and cover until ready to serve.

Spelt toasts

100 g spelt grain

1 tablespoon dried yeast

250 g spelt flour

½ teaspoon sea salt

plain flour, for dusting

Makes about 40 toasts

Put the spelt in a sieve and rinse well under cold running water. Put it in a saucepan with 1 litre water and bring to the boil. Reduce the heat to low, cover with a lid and cook for 45 minutes. Remove the lid and boil rapidly until almost all the liquid has evaporated. Meanwhile, put the yeast in a small bowl with 4 tablespoons warm water, stir, cover and leave to rest in a warm place until the mixture is frothy. While it is still warm, put the spelt in a bowl with the spelt flour, salt, 250 ml tepid water and the yeast and stir to bring the mixture together to form a sticky dough. Put the dough on a lightly floured work surface and gently knead for 1 minute. Carefully transfer the dough to a lightly oiled bowl, cover with a tea towel and leave to rise in a warm place for 1–1¼ hours, until it has risen and doubled in size.

Preheat the oven to 200°C (400°F) Gas 6. Tip the dough out onto a lightly oiled baking tray and, using floured hands, form the dough into a loaf about 20 x 10 cm, tapering at the ends. Bake the bread in the preheated oven for 40 minutes. Carefully slide the loaf off the tray and directly onto the oven shelf, then bake for a further 5 minutes. Remove from the oven and leave to cool. To serve, slice into ½-cm wide pieces and toast under a hot grill until golden on both sides.

Salmon rillettes with Melba toast

A rillette is a very traditional way of potting and preserving meats, such as pork or duck, in fat. Here is a lighter, healthier and fuss-free version of this French classic. Some recipes call for the salmon to be steamed or poached, then flaked and mixed in with the other ingredients, but here it is simply cooked in a paper parcel which traps all the healthy oils and retains more flavour with tasty results.

300 g salmon fillet (smoked if liked), skinned and pin-boned

50 g unsalted butter, chilled and cut into cubes

½ teaspoon sea salt

1 lemon, 1 half sliced and the other juiced

1 tablespoon finely chopped fresh dill

2 tablespoons snipped chives

4 slices of white bread

Serves 4

Preheat the oven to 220°C (425°F) Gas 7.

Put the salmon on a sheet of baking parchment large enough to wrap the fish entirely. Distribute the butter cubes evenly over the fish, sprinkle with the sea salt, add the lemon slices and finish with the dill. Firmly wrap up the fish in the paper, put it on a baking tray and cook in the preheated oven for 10 minutes. Leave in the paper and leave to cool to room temperature.

Remove the fish from the paper and pour any collected oil and juices into a large bowl. Discard the lemon slices. Flake the fish and put it in the bowl with the juices then add the chives and the lemon juice. Cover and refrigerate until needed.

To make the Melba toasts, preheat the grill to high and trim the crusts off the bread. Toast the bread on both sides until golden. Using a serrated knife, carefully cut each slice widthways to make 8 very thin slices. Cut each slice into 4 small triangles, return these to the grill and toast the uncooked side until golden. Serve alongside the salmon rillettes.

3 large red peppers

1 slice of day-old sourdough bread, cut into small pieces

100 g walnut halves, coarsely chopped

½ teaspoon dried chilli flakes

1 tablespoon sun-dried tomato paste

2 garlic cloves, chopped

2 teaspoons freshly squeezed lemon juice

1 tablespoon balsamic vinegar

2 teaspoons caster sugar

1 teaspoon ground cumin

2 tablespoons olive oil, plus extra to serve

chopped pistachios, to sprinkle

sea salt and freshly ground black pepper

toasted flatbread, roughly torn, to serve

Serves 6–8

Cook the peppers one at a time by skewering each one on a fork and holding it directly over a gas flame for about 10–15 minutes, until the skin is blackened all over. Alternatively, put them on a baking tray and then in an oven preheated to 220°C (425°F) Gas 7. Cook them for 10–15 minutes, until the skin has puffed up and blackened all over. Transfer to a bowl, cover with a tea towel and leave until cool enough to handle.

Using your hands, remove the skin and seeds from the peppers and tear the flesh into pieces. Put it in a food processor and add the remaining ingredients. Process to a coarse paste. Season to taste and transfer to a bowl. Cover and refrigerate for at least 8 hours (ideally overnight) to allow the flavours to fully develop.

To serve, bring the dip to room temperature and transfer it to a bowl. Drizzle with olive oil and sprinkle with chopped pistachios. Serve with toasted flatbreads. It will keep in an airtight container in the refrigerator for 4–5 days.

Roasted red pepper and walnut dip with flatbread

This is a traditional Syrian dip called muhammara. There it would be served as part of a meze selection, with houmous, aubergine dip (baba ganoush), pickles, olives, cheese and flatbreads. It's perfect for entertaining, as it benefits from being made a day in advance. Any left over can be used as a spooning sauce to serve with grilled fish or lamb.

500 ml extra virgin olive oil

1 sprig of fresh oregano

2 teaspoons finely chopped fresh flat-leaf parsley leaves

6 very ripe tomatoes, ideally Roma

½ teaspoon sea salt

200 g soft goats' cheese

1 small baguette

2 garlic cloves, peeled

Serves 4

Preheat the oven to 130°C (250°F) Gas ½.

Put the oil in a small, non-reactive baking dish. Add the oregano and parsley. Cut the tomatoes in half and arrange them in a single layer in the dish. Ideally you want the tomatoes to be almost fully submerged in the oil. Sprinkle the salt evenly over the tomatoes.

Cook in the preheated oven for about 5 hours, until the tomatoes are intensely red and softened, yet still retain their shape. Remove from the oven and leave the tomatoes in the oil to cool completely.

Put the goats' cheese in a serving bowl. Preheat the grill. Slice the baguette very thinly. Toast the bread on both sides until golden and crisp and rub one side with the peeled garlic cloves.

Remove the tomatoes from the oil and arrange them on a serving platter with the cheese and garlic toasts on the side. Let your guests help themselves.

Slow-cooked tomatoes with goats' cheese and garlic toasts

Oven-roasted tomatoes are so simple to prepare that it's easy to forget just how good they taste when done well! This is a very slow-cooked version, almost like a confit. Do use in-season tomatoes for a sweet, heady flavour that works well here with the tart goats' cheese.

Garlic-infused olive oil, warm marinated olives and serrano ham platter

This sharing plate is simplicity itself to put together and absolutely no preparation is needed once your guests arrive. Lay out the platter and let it sit at room temperature for a short while before serving.

Garlic-infused olive oil

8 garlic cloves, unpeeled

65 ml light olive oil

65 ml extra virgin olive oil

2 tablespoons balsamic vinegar

Warm marinated olives

100 g large green olives, such as Sicilian

100 g small black olives, such as Ligurian

250 ml extra virgin olive oil

2 sprigs of fresh thyme

2 dried red chillies

1 bay leaf

2 thin slices of orange peel

8 slices of jamón serrano (Spanish salted, air-dried ham)

good crusty bread, to serve

Serves 6–8

To make the garlic-infused olive oil, put the garlic cloves and light olive oil in a small saucepan and cook over medium heat for 5 minutes. Remove from the heat and leave to cool. Add the extra virgin olive oil and vinegar and transfer to a serving bowl.

Put the olives in a small, heatproof bowl. Put the oil, thyme, chillies, bay leaf and orange peel in a small saucepan. Set over medium heat. As soon as you hear the herbs starting to sizzle in the oil, remove the pan from the heat and pour the mixture over the olives. Leave to cool for 20 minutes.

To serve, arrange the garlic-infused oil, olives, jamón and bread on a platter and let your guests help themselves.

Sesame prawn toasts with pickled carrot

When entertaining it helps if you think of yourself as a caterer and use some tricks of the trade. Dishes that can be made ahead of time are very useful – the prawn mixture here can be 'prepped' several hours in advance and the toasts simply cooked to order.

300 g raw peeled and deveined prawns

6 spring onions, finely chopped

1 tablespoon finely grated fresh ginger

2 teaspoons dry sherry (optional)

1 teaspoon light soy sauce

1 egg white, lightly beaten

6 thick slices of white bread

50 g sesame seeds

sea salt

about 250 ml vegetable oil, for shallow frying

sprigs of fresh coriander, to garnish

Pickled carrot

1 large carrot, coarsely grated

2 tablespoons Japanese pickled ginger, sliced

2 tablespoons juice from the pickled ginger jar

½ teaspoon caster sugar

2 shallots, thinly sliced on the diagonal

Makes 24

To make the pickled carrot, combine the carrot, pickled ginger, pickled ginger juice, sugar and shallots in a small, non-reactive bowl. Set aside until needed.

Put the prawns, spring onions, ginger, sherry, soy sauce, egg white and some salt in a food processor. Process until roughly chopped.

Trim the crusts off the bread and discard or save for another use. Cut each slice into 4 triangles. Put the sesame seeds on a plate. Spread about 2 teaspoons of the prawn mixture onto each piece of bread, pressing down lightly. Press each triangle into the sesame seeds to lightly coat.

Put the oil in a shallow frying pan and heat over medium/high heat. Add a piece of bread to test if the oil is ready – if the bread sizzles on contact, the oil is hot enough. Use a fish slice to carefully add the prawn toasts to the pan, prawn-side down, and cook for 1 minute. Turn over and cook for 1 minute more, until golden. Transfer to a plate covered with kitchen paper to absorb the excess oil. Spoon a little pickled carrot over the top of each toast and add a sprig of coriander. Serve immediately.

Chilli salt squid

We really ought to eat more squid; it is cheap and in plentiful supply. Fresh squid can look a little scary, but it really is superior to the frozen stuff. It should be cooked in one of two ways: very quickly or for a long time – anywhere in between makes it tough.

400 g cleaned squid (1 large tube)

2 tablespoons cornflour

1 tablespoon plain flour

½ teaspoon ground white pepper

½ teaspoon mild chilli powder

3 teaspoons sea salt

1 large fresh red chilli, deseeded and thinly sliced

a small handful of fresh coriander leaves, chopped

vegetable oil, for deep-frying

lemon wedges, to serve

Serves 4

Cut the squid tube down one side so that it opens up. Use a sharp knife to trim and discard any internal membranes. Cut it lengthways into 2-cm wide strips, then cut each strip in half. Combine the cornflour, plain flour, pepper, chilli powder and salt in a large bowl. Half-fill a saucepan with the vegetable oil and heat over high heat until the surface of the oil shimmers.

Toss half of the squid pieces in the flour mixture, quickly shaking off the excess, and add them to the oil. Cook for about 2 minutes, until deep golden. Remove with a slotted spoon and drain on kitchen paper. Repeat with the remaining squid.

Add the chilli slices to the oil and cook for just a few seconds. Remove from the pan and drain on kitchen paper. Put the squid and chilli on a serving plate and sprinkle with the coriander. Serve while still warm with plenty of lemon wedges on the side for squeezing.

Potato crisps with soured cream and caviar dip

This recipe takes the humble potato to new heights. Gourmet crisps are made using firm, waxy potatoes which gives them a lovely golden colour and buttery flavour. They are good enough to enjoy on their own but a real treat served this way. You don't have to buy expensive caviar – salmon pearls (roe) are just as good; it's the salty flavour burst followed by the creamy indulgence of soured cream that's delicious.

800 g Kipfler potatoes (about 8) or other small waxy potato

125 ml olive oil

125 ml vegetable oil

250 ml soured cream or crème fraîche

1 tablespoon snipped chives

2–3 tablespoons caviar or salmon roe

sea salt flakes, to sprinkle

Serves 6–8

Cut the potatoes into slices about 2–3 mm thick. Bring a large saucepan of lightly salted water to the boil. Add the potatoes, cover the pan with a lid and remove from the heat. Leave in the hot water for 5 minutes. Drain well and arrange the potatoes on a wire rack in a single layer until completely cool.

Put the oils in a saucepan or large frying pan and set over high heat. When the oil is hot, cook the potato slices in batches for 5–6 minutes each, turning once or twice with tongs, until crisp and golden. Remove from the oil using a metal slotted spoon and drain on kitchen paper.

Put the crisps in a serving bowl, sprinkle liberally with sea salt flakes and toss to coat. Combine the soured cream and chives in a small bowl, top with the caviar and serve with the warm crisps on the side for dipping.

Toasted mozzarella and basil fingers

These cheesy snacks are great served with chilled white wine or beer. If you have trouble sourcing smoked mozzarella, simply substitute buffalo mozzarella or even a strongly flavoured fontina. For a spicy treat, try replacing the basil with a little smoked chilli jelly, available from gourmet retailers.

8 thin slices of white bread

200 g mozzarella cheese, preferably smoked

a large handful of shredded basil leaves

4 tablespoons olive oil

sea salt and freshly ground black pepper

Makes 16–20

Trim any larger crusts off the bread without being too fussy. Lay 4 slices of the bread on a work surface and divide the cheese and basil on top. Add a slice of bread to each.

Preheat a large, non-stick frying pan over medium heat and add 2 tablespoons of the olive oil. Arrange the sandwiches in the pan and drizzle the remaining oil over the top slices of bread.

Cook for 2–3 minutes, using a spatula to gently press down on the sandwiches. Turn over and cook for a further 2 minutes.

Transfer to a chopping board and cut each sandwich into 4–5 thin fingers. Season with a little salt and pepper and serve immediately while the mozzarella is still molten.

Polenta chips with green Tabasco mayonnaise

These 'chips' made from polenta make a more sophisticated nibble than traditional potato chips. They are delicious served hot with a spicy Tabasco mayonnaise but any hot dip or salsa makes a good accompaniment.

1 litre chicken or vegetable stock

250 g instant polenta

25 g butter

50 g Parmesan, finely grated

250 ml vegetable oil

125 ml light olive oil

30 g plain flour

125 ml mayonnaise

2 teaspoons green Tabasco sauce

2 baking trays, lightly oiled

Makes about 60

Put the stock in a saucepan and bring to the boil. While the stock is boiling, pour in the polenta in a steady stream and whisk until it is all incorporated. Continue whisking for about 2 minutes, until the mixture is thick and smooth. Remove from the heat and stir in the butter and Parmesan. Spoon half of the mixture into each of the prepared baking trays. Use the back of a metal spoon to smooth the top. Cover and refrigerate for at least 4 hours, until firm.

Transfer the polenta to a chopping board. Trim the edges. Cut the block lengthways in half – then cut it into 1-cm thick slices, to make about 60 chips.

Pour the oils into a frying pan and heat over medium/high heat. The oil is ready if a small piece of the polenta mixture sizzles on contact. Put about one quarter of the chips in a colander and sprinkle over some of the flour. Add these to the oil and cook for 4–5 minutes, turning often, until golden. Transfer the cooked chips to a plate covered with kitchen paper to absorb the excess oil. Cover with foil and keep warm in a low oven while you cook the rest. Repeat with the other chips.

Mix the mayonnaise and Tabasco together in a bowl and serve with the hot chips on the side for dipping.

Spicy chilli bean dip

Black beans are popular in Latin American cooking. They are left whole in this recipe but you could roughly mash after cooking to make them more gooey if preferred.

440 g dried black beans

2 tablespoons olive oil

1 red onion, chopped

4 garlic cloves, chopped

1 red pepper, deseeded and diced

1 tablespoon ground cumin

2 teaspoons dried oregano, preferably Greek

2 teaspoons chilli powder

2 x 400-g tins chopped tomatoes

a handful of fresh coriander leaves, chopped

natural Greek yoghurt

warmed corn chips, to serve

Serves 6–8

Put the beans in a saucepan with 2 litres cold water. Bring to the boil, reduce the heat to a simmer and cook, uncovered, for about 1½ hours, until just tender and not falling apart. Drain well and set aside.

Heat the oil in a large, heavy-based saucepan set over medium heat. Add the onion, garlic and red pepper and cook for 8–10 minutes, until softened. Stir in the cumin, oregano and chilli powder and fry for 1 minute, until the spices are aromatic.

Increase the heat to high. Add the tomatoes, beans and 250 ml cold water and bring to the boil. Reduce the heat to low, partially cover the pan and cook for 1½–2 hours, adding a little more water from time to time if necessary. Transfer to a serving bowl, top with a dollop of yoghurt and serve with corn chips on the side for dipping.

Houmous

This popular creamy dip is an essential dish at the meze table in many eastern Mediterranean countries. Although now widely available in supermarkets, home-made houmous is always superior.

220 g dried chickpeas

3 tablespoons tahini (sesame seed paste)

2 garlic cloves

2 tablespoons freshly squeezed lemon juice

4 tablespoons olive oil

1 teaspoon ground cumin

paprika, to sprinkle

toasted flatbreads, to serve

Serves 4–6

Put the chickpeas in a large bowl with 1 litre cold water and soak for 6 hours or overnight. Bring a large saucepan of water to the boil. Drain the chickpeas and add to the boiling water. Bring to the boil then reduce the heat to a simmer. Cook, uncovered, for about 1 hour, until very tender. Drain over a bowl, reserving the cooking liquid.

Put the chickpeas and 200 ml of the hot cooking liquid in a food processor with the tahini, garlic, lemon juice and cumin and process until smooth. With the motor running, add 3 tablespoons of the oil until smooth and thick. Transfer to a serving plate, making a well in the centre. Pour the remaining oil into the well and sprinkle over the paprika. Serve with toasted flatbreads on the side for dipping.

Deli-bought Spanish tapas

You can buy everything you need to put together a selection of Spanish-style tapas in a deli or a supermarket these days: fine slices of serrano ham or (even better) Pata Negra (acorn-fed ham), chorizo, thin slices of Manchego cheese, toasted and salted Marcona almonds, large caperberries, marinated olives and piquillo peppers, which taste particularly good warmed through with a little olive oil and garlic.

Simply arrange all of your bought tapas on attractive plates or wooden boards. Your dishes will taste better if served at room temperature, rather than cold from the fridge. Serve with plenty of thinly sliced crusty bread on the side.

A chilled dry sherry makes the perfect accompaniment, or a crisp white wine or light beer if preferred.

Charcuterie and radishes

This is one of the easiest possible starters – which is why so many French bistros serve it. Simply buy some slices of air-dried ham, some whole saucisson and a thick slice of pâté. You could also buy rillettes, which you can transfer to a small pottery bowl and pretend is your own! This is a great starter to serve while you have a casserole cooking in the oven.

Simply arrange all of your bought charcuterie on attractive plates or boards. The meats will taste better if served at room temperature, rather than cold from the fridge.

Wash a couple of bunches of fresh radishes, cutting the leaves off a few centimetres above the base of the stem. Lay on some good French artisanal butter, some crusty baguette and a sharp knife to cut the sausage. Simplicity itself!

Pork and chicken liver terrine with pistachios

Some classics are surprisingly good for modern day entertaining. A terrine can be made well in advance and, once served up, there is no fuss. It's perfect for sharing, so simply provide everyone with a knife and lay out some good bread and dishes of pickled cornichons (baby gherkins) and a spicy fruit chutney.

1 kg pork mince

200 g dry-cured pork lardons

300 g chicken livers, roughly chopped

1 garlic clove, crushed

finely grated zest of 1 orange

2 teaspoons fennel seeds

50 g shelled pistachios

1 egg, beaten

a handful of fresh flat-leaf parsley leaves, finely chopped

12 bacon rashers

cornichons and spiced fruit chutney, to serve

sliced baguette, to serve

a loaf tin or terrine dish, 20 x 10 x 7 cm, lightly oiled

a large, shallow baking dish or roasting tin

Serves 10–12

Put the pork mince, lardons, chicken livers, garlic, orange zest, fennel seeds and pistachios in a mixing bowl. Use your hands to combine thoroughly. Cover and refrigerate for at least 6 hours, preferably overnight, mixing occasionally.

Preheat the oven to 180°C (350°F) Gas 4.

Add the egg to the pork mixture and use your hands to thoroughly combine. Use the bacon rashers to line the loaf tin, ensuring that the ends of the rashers overhang the sides of the tin.

Spoon the pork mixture into the tin, pressing it down into the tin. The filling may be higher than the top of the tin at this stage, but it will settle during cooking. Cover the top of the loaf tin firmly with 2 layers of foil. Put the tin in the large, shallow baking dish or roasting tin. Add enough hot water to come halfway up the sides of the loaf tin.

Cook in the preheated oven for 3 hours.

Remove the terrine from the baking dish and leave it to cool completely, leaving the foil intact. When cool, remove the foil and carefully turn the terrine out onto a serving plate or board. Cover and refrigerate until [...] Serve with the cornichons, [...] crusty baguette.

trout, celeriac salad

Here is a simple combination of ingredients that meld together to make a deliciously fresh-tasting salad. It's a salad in the coleslaw sense of the word and is best eaten spooned onto crisp little toasts.

200 g celeriac, peeled and grated

185 ml mayonnaise

1 tablespoon freshly squeezed lemon juice

1 smoked trout fillet (about 300 g)

2 sweet eating apples, cut into wedges

2 teaspoons finely chopped tarragon

2 tablespoons finely chopped fresh flat-leaf parsley

½ teaspoon Spanish smoked paprika (pimentón dulce)

1 baguette, to serve

Serves 4–6

Combine the celeriac, mayonnaise and lemon juice in a bowl.

Peel the skin from the trout and discard. Roughly flake the fish into a separate mixing bowl. Add the apple wedges, tarragon, parsley, paprika and the celeriac mixture. Gently toss to combine without breaking up the fish too much. Spoon into a serving bowl.

Preheat the grill. Finely slice the baguette. Toast on both sides until golden. Serve alongside the salad.

2 pitta breads

125 ml olive oil

1 smoked trout (about 450–500 g)

1 small head of cos lettuce, shredded

1 large cucumber, cut into thin batons

4 Roma tomatoes, halved and sliced

1 small red onion, thinly sliced

a large handful of fresh flat-leaf parsley leaves, roughly chopped

a handful of fresh mint leaves, roughly chopped

3 tablespoons freshly squeezed lemon juice

2 teaspoons ground sumac (optional) or freshly ground black pepper

Serves 4–6

Preheat the oven to 180°C (350°F) Gas 4.

Split the pitta breads in half and brush lightly with some of the olive oil. Put on a baking tray and cook in the preheated oven for about 10 minutes, turning after 5 minutes, until golden. While still warm, break the bread into smaller pieces and set aside on a wire rack to cool and crisp up.

Carefully pull the skin off the trout and discard. Gently fork the flesh from the bones and flake into smaller pieces.

Put the lettuce, cucumber, tomato, onion and herbs in a large salad bowl. Add the trout and pitta bread pieces and gently toss to combine, being careful not to break up the trout too much.

Put the remaining olive oil in a small bowl. Add the lemon juice and whisk with a fork to combine. Pour the dressing over the salad and sprinkle with a little sumac, if using, or a few grinds of black pepper. Serve immediately.

Smoked trout fattoush

Fattoush is a fresh-tasting salad from the Lebanon. Despite its exotic name, the ingredients are basically summer garden produce – cucumber, tomato, parsley and mint – with the addition of crisp pieces of toasted pitta bread. All these foods work well with the delicate taste of smoked trout. This is perfect served either as a starter or a light summer lunch.

Thai-style beef with tomato and herb salad

Thai cuisine features some great meat-based salads that are wonderfully zingy and refreshing. The amount of chilli you use is up to you. You can leave out the toasted chillies and only use fresh ones if you like, but the smoky flavour they give it is very good.

2 tablespoons Thai fragrant rice

1 teaspoon crushed fresh chillies

1–2 thick slices of rump steak (about 900 g in total and about 2 cm thick), trimmed of any fat

1½ tablespoons sunflower or light olive oil

3–4 teaspoons caster sugar

freshly squeezed juice of 3 limes

4 tablespoons Thai fish sauce

2 large garlic cloves, grated

2–3 medium-hot fresh red chillies, deseeded and very finely chopped

8 small shallots, very thinly sliced or a bunch of spring onions, trimmed and thinly sliced

5 heaped tablespoons chopped coriander leaves

3 heaped tablespoons chopped mint leaves

250 g cherry tomatoes, quartered

1 cos lettuce heart, washed and crisped in the fridge

a ridged grill pan

Serves 6–8

Heat a small frying pan over medium heat, add the rice and cook, stirring occasionally until golden and fragrant (about 5 minutes). Take off the heat, allow to cool for a couple of minutes, then grind in a mortar with a pestle or the end of a rolling pin. Toast the crushed chillies in the same way for a few seconds, add to the rice and grind again. Heat a ridged grill pan for about 3 minutes until smoking hot, rub the steak with the oil and cook for about 1½ minutes each side until charred but still rare (or longer if you prefer). Set aside to cool while you make the dressing.

Dissolve the sugar in the lime juice, add the fish sauce, the garlic and half the chopped chillies and taste. Add more fish sauce and chillies if you think the dressing needs it and a little water if the dressing is too strong.

Slice the steak thinly, then tip the slices (together with any juices) into a bowl with the dressing and add the shallots, coriander, mint and tomatoes. Toss, then sprinkle with the toasted rice and chilli mixture. Finely shred the cos lettuce and arrange the shredded leaves on a large platter. Top with the dressed beef and serve immediately.

Prawn and cucumber sesame noodles

This is a clean, refreshing noodle salad that works as both a light lunch or supper dish.

250 g fine rice or dried soba noodles

400 g cooked shelled prawns, thawed if frozen

⅔ cucumber, peeled, quartered, deseeded and cut into diagonal slices

½ bunch of spring onions, trimmed and thinly sliced

Dressing

6 tablespoons Japanese seasoned rice vinegar

2 tablespoons light soy sauce

4 tablespoons sunflower or rapeseed oil

2 tablespoons sesame oil

1½ teaspoons finely grated fresh ginger or ginger paste

1½ teaspoons finely grated garlic or garlic paste

4 tablespoons sesame seeds

5 tablespoons finely chopped fresh coriander leaves

sea salt (optional)

Serves 6–8

Break the dried noodles into thirds and put them in a heatproof bowl. Pour over boiling water, leave for 3 minutes, then drain and rinse under cold water. Put them in a large serving bowl and add the prawns, cucumber and spring onions.

To toast the sesame seeds, warm them in a dry frying pan over low heat until they begin to change colour. Set aside until you are ready to use them.

Pour the rice vinegar and soy sauce into a separate bowl, then whisk in the sunflower and sesame oils. Stir in the ginger and garlic, add the dressing to the noodles and toss everything together. Check the seasoning, adding a little salt if necessary. Just before serving, sprinkle over the toasted sesame seeds and chopped coriander and toss again.

Roast chicken and minted tabbouleh salad

130 g bulghur wheat

1 rotisserie chicken

a large handful each of fresh mint, flat-leaf parsley and coriander leaves, finely chopped

3 Roma tomatoes, halved

2 cucumbers, chopped

2 Little Gem lettuces, washed and leaves separated

2 tablespoons freshly squeezed lemon juice

65 ml olive oil

sea salt and freshly ground black pepper

wholemeal pitta breads, to serve (optional)

Serves 4

Thankfully, free-range, organic rotisserie chickens are now readily available in larger supermarkets. They are a great time-saver when you are entertaining. Shred the flesh and use in soups, pie fillings (see Chicken Pot Pies on page 89) or in a substantial main course salad, as here.

Put the bulghur wheat in a heatproof bowl and pour in 185 ml boiling water. Cover and set aside for 15 minutes. Stir well with a fork to fluff the grains up and tip into a larger bowl.

Shred the meat and skin, if liked, of the chicken and put it in the bowl with the bulghur wheat. Add the herbs, tomatoes, cucumber and lettuce.

Put the lemon juice and olive oil in a small bowl and whisk with a fork to combine. Pour over the salad. Season to taste with salt and pepper and toss to combine all the ingredients.

Serve immediately with warmed wholemeal pitta breads on the side, if liked.

Pasta salad with tuna, chilli and rocket

400 g large dried pasta shells, such as lumaconi

65 ml olive oil

2 red onions, finely chopped

2 garlic cloves, finely chopped

1 large red chilli, deseeded and finely chopped

2 tablespoons small salted capers, rinsed

1 tablespoon red wine vinegar

400-g tin or jar tuna chunks in oil, well drained

50 g feta cheese, crumbled

50 g wild rocket

sea salt and freshly ground black pepper

lemon wedges, to serve

Serves 4

Tinned fish sometimes gets a bad press but it is one of the most convenient and healthy fast foods to have on hand. It it lovely with other simple, fresh Mediterranean flavours, such as lemon and parsley. The inclusion of feta cheese in this salad may seem a little odd, but it really does work. Just a small amount provides an extra tangy, savoury element to this summery pasta dish. Any large, open pasta shape will work, but lumaconi are used here, which translated from the Italian means 'big snail shells'.

Bring a large saucepan of lightly salted water to the boil. Add the pasta shells and cook for 8–10 minutes, until tender. Drain well and add 1 tablespoon of the olive oil. Transfer to a large serving bowl.

Heat the remaining oil in a large frying pan set over high heat. Add the onions, garlic, chilli and capers and cook, stirring, for 2–3 minutes, until the onion has softened. Add the vinegar and cook for 1 further minute. Add the tuna and use a fork to roughly break up any larger chunks, without mushing the tuna too much.

Add the tuna mixture to the bowl with the pasta. Add the feta and rocket and gently toss to combine. Season to taste with salt and a generous amount of freshly ground black pepper.

Serve warm or cold, as liked, with lemon wedges for squeezing.

...d with ...ns

...is a slight twist on a classic Greek salad. Butter beans are a staple of Greek cuisine but are usually served baked in a tomato sauce. Their delicate flavour works here with tangy feta cheese and olives. Let sit at room temperature for half an hour before serving.

400 g cherry tomatoes, halved

50 g kalamata olives, halved and stoned

leaves from a small bunch of fresh mint, chopped

leaves from a small bunch of fresh flat-leaf parsley, chopped

2 x 410-g tins butter beans, drained and well rinsed

3 tablespoons extra virgin olive oil

2 red onions, thinly sliced

2 garlic cloves, finely chopped

3 tablespoons freshly squeezed lemon juice

200 g feta cheese, cubed

sea salt and freshly ground black pepper

toasted ciabatta or similar, to serve

Serves 4

Put the tomatoes, olives, mint, parsley and beans in a large bowl and toss to combine.

Put the oil in a frying pan and set over medium heat. Add the onions and garlic. When they start to sizzle in the oil, remove from the heat and pour over the tomato mixture. Stir in the lemon juice and add the feta. Season to taste with salt and pepper and toss well to combine.

Serve at room temperature with slices of toasted ciabatta.

Farmers' market salad with goats' cheese, asparagus and roast beetroot

This is a good recipe to have up your sleeve if you visit your local farmers' market regularly. Don't let memories of pickled, vinegar-soused beetroot put you off – roast beetroot has a sweet, earthy flavour that just needs a few salad leaves and some fresh, tangy white goats' cheese to set it off to perfection.

a bunch of fresh beetroot

4 tablespoons sunflower oil

800 g broad bean pods

a bunch of fresh asparagus

3 tablespoons rice vinegar

2 tablespoons walnut oil

100 g mixed salad leaves, such as rocket, watercress or baby spinach

200 g goats' cheese

a small handful of freshly chopped green herbs, such as parsley or dill

a few fresh chives, snipped

sea salt and freshly ground black pepper

crusty bread, to serve

Serves 4–6

Preheat the oven to 200°C (400°F) Gas 6.

Cut off the beetroot tops and trim off the roots. Wash the beetroot under running water to remove any dirt and dry with kitchen paper. Take a large piece of kitchen foil and place it on a baking tray. Oil it lightly, place the beetroot in the centre and scrunch the edges of the foil together to make a loose parcel. Cook in the preheated oven for about 50 minutes–1 hour, until tender. When cool enough to handle, peel off the skins and cut into quarters or smaller wedges.

Meanwhile, pod the broad beans and cook them in boiling water for about 8–10 minutes, until just cooked. When cool enough to handle,

pop the beans out of their skins. Cut the tips of the asparagus off about a third of the way down the stalk and steam for about 3–4 minutes until just tender. Set aside and let cool.

Shake the vinegar, oils, salt and pepper together in a screw-top glass jar. Use half to lightly dress the beetroot. Divide the leaves between 4 serving plates and drizzle with a little of the remaining dressing. Arrange the beetroot wedges over the leaves and top with chunks of goats' cheese and the broad beans. Scatter over the herbs, drizzle over the remaining dressing and grind a little black pepper over the top.

Serve immediately with some crusty bread.

Pumpkin soup with honey and sage

This is based on a delicious soup that is served at a restaurant in London called Tom's Kitchen, run by top chef Tom Aikens. His version contains chicken stock, but this recipe is vegetarian. You could base it on chicken stock too if preferred.

75 g unsalted butter

1 small onion, chopped

1 carrot, finely chopped

1 garlic clove, crushed

1 kg pumpkin or butternut squash, deseeded, peeled and cut into cubes

2 tablespoons clear honey

3 sprigs of fresh sage, plus extra crisp-fried leaves (optional), to serve

750 ml vegetable stock

75 ml double cream

freshly squeezed lemon juice, to taste

sea salt and freshly ground black pepper

wholemeal or multigrain bread, to serve

Serves 4–6

Gently melt the butter in a large lidded saucepan or flameproof casserole. Add the onion, carrot and garlic, stir, cover and cook over low heat for about 4–5 minutes. Add the cubed pumpkin, honey and sage, stir, replace the lid and continue to cook very gently for about 10 minutes. Pour in the stock, bring to the boil and cook for a further 10 minutes until the vegetables are soft. Turn off the heat and allow the soup to cool slightly, then remove the sage and strain the soup, retaining the liquid. Put half the cooked vegetables in a food processor with just enough of the reserved cooking liquid to blend into a smooth purée.

Transfer to a clean saucepan and repeat with the remaining vegetables, adding the purée to the first batch. Whizz the remaining liquid in the food processor to pick up the last bits of purée and add that too. Bring the soup slowly to the boil, then stir in the cream without boiling further. Season to taste with lemon juice (about 1 tablespoon), salt (about 1 teaspoon) and pepper.

Serve with an extra swirl of cream or scatter some crisp-fried sage leaves on top and serve with wholemeal or multigrain bread.

Roasted tomato soup with rarebit toasts

Many Mediterranean dishes feature tomatoes and few other ingredients, so it's essential that the tomatoes themselves taste good. Choose the ripest, tastiest tomatoes you can find for this rich soup and you will not be disappointed.

1 kg Italian tomatoes, such as Roma, halved

2 small red onions, quartered

6 sprigs of fresh lemon thyme

1 teaspoon sugar

1 teaspoon sea salt

2 garlic cloves, sliced

2 tablespoons olive oil

500 ml vegetable stock

sea salt and freshly ground black pepper

Rarebit toasts

100 g mature Cheddar

3 tablespoons wheat beer

1 tablespoon Worcestershire sauce

4 slices of baguette or similar

Serves 4

Preheat the oven to 170°C (325°F) Gas 3.

Put the tomatoes, onion, lemon thyme, sugar, salt, garlic and oil in a large bowl. Use your hands to toss the ingredients to combine and evenly coat them in the oil. Tip the mixture out onto a baking tray and roast in the preheated oven for 1½ hours. Discard the lemon thyme sprigs then put the tomatoes, onions and any tasty juices in a food processor or blender and process until smooth, adding a little stock if the mixture is too thick to process. Transfer to a large saucepan, add the stock and cook over gentle heat for 10 minutes. Season to taste and keep warm.

Preheat the grill to high. Put the Cheddar, beer and Worcestershire sauce in a small saucepan set over low heat. Stir until the cheese has melted and the mixture is smooth. Toast the bread under the preheated grill on one side only. Spread about 2 tablespoons of the cheese mixture on each untoasted side of bread and grill until it is bubbling and golden.

Ladle the soup into 4 warmed serving bowls, put a rarebit toast on top of each one and serve immediately.

Sweet potato and coconut soup with Thai pesto

Sweet potatoes take on a velvety, creamy texture when blended so are excellent in soups. Here, their sweetness is cut through with some spicy Asian flavours in the form of a Thai-style peanut pesto.

1 tablespoon light olive oil

500 g sweet potato, peeled and chopped into chunks

1 red onion, chopped

1 tablespoon Thai red curry paste

500 ml vegetable stock

500 ml coconut milk

Thai pesto

100 g unsalted peanuts, lightly toasted

2 garlic cloves, chopped

2 teaspoons finely grated fresh ginger

2 large green chillies, deseeded and chopped

1 small bunch of fresh coriander

1 large handful of fresh mint leaves

1 large handful of fresh basil leaves

2 tablespoons Thai fish sauce or light soy sauce

2 tablespoons freshly squeezed lime juice

1 tablespoon soft light brown sugar

Serves 4

Put the oil in a heavy-based saucepan and set over medium heat. Add the sweet potato and onion, partially cover with a lid and cook for 15 minutes, stirring often, until soft and just starting to turn golden.

Increase the heat to high, add the curry paste and stir-fry with the sweet potato for 3–4 minutes so that the paste cooks and becomes fragrant. Add the stock and coconut milk and bring to the boil. Transfer the mixture to a blender and whizz until smooth. Return the soup to a clean saucepan and put on a low simmer just to keep warm.

To make the pesto, put all of the ingredients in a food processor or blender and whizz, occasionally scraping down the sides of the bowl, until you have a chunky green paste and the ingredients are all evenly chopped. Ladle the soup into 4 warmed serving bowls. Top with a generous spoonful of Thai pesto and serve immediately. Any leftover pesto can be served on the side.

effortless mains

Spicy pork curry with lemon rice

It's useful to have a curry recipe to hand that does not require a vast number of different spices. With the exception of the ground cumin, the curry paste that forms the basis of this recipe calls for fresh ingredients. If pork is not your thing, simply replace it with the same quantity of a stewing steak like chuck – the cooking time will be the same.

2 tomatoes, chopped

2 fresh green chillies, chopped

4 garlic cloves

1 onion, chopped

2 teaspoons ground cumin

a 5-cm piece of fresh ginger, peeled and grated

a small bunch of fresh coriander

2 tablespoons vegetable oil

750 g pork shoulder, cut into bite-sized pieces

2 tablespoons white vinegar

shredded fresh ginger, to garnish

Lemon rice

400 g basmati rice

½ teaspoon ground turmeric

3 tablespoons unsalted butter

4–6 dried curry leaves

½ teaspoon brown mustard seeds

2 teaspoons finely grated lemon zest

1 tablespoon freshly squeezed lemon juice

a flameproof casserole (optional)

Serves 4

Put the tomatoes, chillies, garlic, onion, cumin, ginger, coriander leaves and stalks (reserving a few leaves to garnish) and oil in a food processor and process until smooth. Put the paste in a flameproof casserole or large heavy-based saucepan and set over medium heat. Cook for 5 minutes, stirring, until aromatic.

Put the pork in the casserole, add 1 litre water and bring to the boil, stirring occasionally. Reduce the heat to low and gently simmer, uncovered, for 1½ hours, stirring often so that the meat doesn't catch and burn. Stir in the vinegar.

Meanwhile, to make the lemon rice, rinse the rice in several changes of cold water. Bring a large saucepan of water to the boil and add the turmeric. Add the rice and cook for 10–12 minutes, until tender. Drain well and return to the warm pan. Heat the butter in a small saucepan set over high heat and cook the curry leaves and mustard seeds until they start to sizzle. Add to the rice along with the lemon zest and juice and stir well to combine.

To serve, garnish the curry with shredded ginger and the reserved coriander leaves and serve with the lemon rice.

Fresh tomato, pea and paneer curry

Southern Indian food tends to have a greater emphasis on fresh ingredients, with just one or two spices thrown in, so this style of cooking is perfect for fuss-free entertaining. Paneer is a firm, white cheese from India – if you can't find it, Cypriot halloumi will work just as well.

2 tablespoons vegetable oil

250 g paneer or halloumi, cubed

1 tablespoon unsalted butter

2 onions, finely chopped

a 5-cm piece of fresh ginger, grated

2 fresh green chillies, deseeded and finely chopped

3 ripe tomatoes, roughly chopped

2 teaspoons white wine vinegar

200 g frozen peas

½ teaspoon garam masala

a handful of fresh coriander leaves

sea salt and freshly ground black pepper

To serve

cooked basmati rice

naan breads

sweet mango chutney

Serves 4

Heat the oil in a frying pan set over medium heat. Add the cubed paneer and cook for 4–5 minutes, turning often, until golden all over. Remove from the pan with a fish slice and put on a plate lined with paper towels to drain away any excess oil.

Add the butter to the pan. When it is melted and sizzling, add the onions and stir-fry until softened and lightly golden. Add the ginger and chillies and cook for 1 minute.

Add the tomatoes, vinegar and 65 ml cold water and bring to the boil. Cook for about 5 minutes, until the sauce has thickened slightly. Add the peas and return the paneer to the pan. Reduce the heat and simmer, uncovered, for about 5 minutes, until the peas are tender.

Stir in the garam masala and season to taste with salt and pepper. Sprinkle the coriander leaves over the top and serve with basmati rice, warmed naan breads and a sweet mango chutney.

Lemon harissa chicken with oven-roasted vegetables

North African flavours are exciting and exotic, but the cooking techniques are often surprisingly simple and quick. Preserved lemons are used extensively in Moroccan cooking and are whole lemons packed in jars with salt. The interesting thing is that you eat only the rind, which contains the essential flavour of the lemon, rather than the flesh. They are available from some larger supermarkets and specialist retailers, so worth tracking down. Any leftover chicken makes a good sandwich filling with some mayonnaise and rocket, but don't assume there will be any leftovers!

a large handful each of fresh coriander, mint and flat-leaf parsley leaves

2 garlic cloves

3 small fresh red chillies, deseeded

½ teaspoon ground cumin

1 tablespoon chopped preserved lemon

4 tablespoons olive oil

6 chicken thigh fillets, halved

1 medium aubergine, cut into large cubes

2 courgettes, thickly sliced

1 small red pepper, quartered and deseeded

1 red onion, cut into thin wedges

2 tablespoons freshly squeezed lemon juice

sea salt and freshly ground black pepper

couscous, to serve (optional)

lemon wedges, to serve

Serves 4

Preheat the oven to 220°C (425°F) Gas 7.

Put the herbs, garlic, chillies, cumin, preserved lemon, 1 tablespoon of the oil and a little salt and pepper in a food processor and process until finely chopped. Put the chicken in a non-reactive bowl, add the herb mixture and toss to coat the chicken. Cover and refrigerate while you cook the vegetables.

Put 2 tablespoons of the olive oil in a roasting tin and put it in the oven for 10 minutes to heat up. Put the aubergine, courgettes, red pepper and onion in the hot roasting tin and season well with salt and pepper. Cook in the preheated oven for 40 minutes, shaking the pan and turning the vegetables after about 20 minutes. Remove from the oven and cover with foil to keep warm while you cook the chicken.

Heat the remaining oil in a frying pan set over medium heat. Put the chicken in the pan and reserve the marinade in the bowl.

Cook the chicken for 7–8 minutes, until a golden crust forms, spooning the reserved marinade over the top. Turn over and cook for 5 minutes, until cooked through. Pour the lemon juice over the chicken and turn the chicken over in the pan.

Arrange the vegetables and chicken on a serving plate. Serve with couscous, if liked, and lemon wedges on the side for squeezing.

Chicken pot pies

The filling for these comforting pies is made with a ready-cooked rotisserie chicken (now available at most large supermarkets). These pies can be made up in advance and kept in the fridge until you are ready to cook them - great for after-work entertaining.

1 small rotisserie chicken

3 tablespoons unsalted butter

1 leek, sliced

1 carrot, diced

1 celery stick, diced

125 ml dry white wine

3 tablespoons plain flour

500 ml chicken stock

100 g frozen peas

125 ml single cream

1 sheet ready-rolled puff pastry, defrosted if frozen

1 egg yolk, beaten with 1 tablespoon water

sea salt and freshly ground black pepper

4 individual baking dishes, each about 250 ml capacity

Serves 4

Preheat the oven to 180°C (350°F) Gas 4.

Remove the skin from the chicken, slice the meat off the bones and chop finely. Set aside until needed.

Melt the butter in a large saucepan set over high heat and add the leek, carrot and celery. Sauté for 5 minutes, until softened. Add the wine and cook for a further 5 minutes, until it has almost evaporated. Add the chicken and stir well to combine. Sprinkle the flour into the pan. Cook for 1 minute, then gradually pour in the stock, stirring constantly as you do so. Bring to the boil and cook uncovered, stirring often, for 2–3 minutes, until the mixture has thickened. Add the peas and cream to the pan and stir well.

Cook for 1 minute, then remove from the heat. Season to taste with salt and pepper and leave to cool to room temperature.

Spoon the mixture into the baking dishes. Unroll the pastry and lay it on a lightly floured work surface. Use a sharp knife to cut circles from the pastry just slightly larger than the top of the dishes.

Put a pastry circle on top of each dish, folding the pastry over the side and pressing down firmly with the tines of a fork. Brush with the egg wash and cook in the preheated oven for about 25–30 minutes, until the pastry is puffed and golden. Serve hot.

...sage, fennel and haricot bean stew

...cal butcher for organic gourmet sausages for this recipe. Haricot beans are small, white oval beans, often used in French cooking, that become very tender when cooked, but cannellini beans would work just as well if that's what you have to hand. This is delicious served with mashed potatoes, soft buttery polenta, or crusty bread – basically something to mop up the delicious sauce. This is a great comfort food dish, perfect for serving to friends for a casual weekend dinner.

2 tablespoons olive oil

12 small pork sausages

1 onion, chopped

1 fennel bulb, chopped

2 garlic cloves, chopped

½ teaspoon fennel seeds

410-g tin haricot or cannellini beans, drained and rinsed

400-g tin chopped tomatoes

2 teaspoons brown sugar

sea salt and freshly ground black pepper

soft polenta or mashed potatoes, to serve

Serves 4

Heat the oil in a large, heavy-based frying pan set over medium heat. Add half of the sausages to the pan and cook for 4–5 minutes, turning often, until well browned all over. Remove from the pan and repeat with the remaining sausages.

Add the onion, fennel, garlic and fennel seeds to the pan and stir-fry for 5 minutes, until the fennel is softened and golden.

Add the beans, tomatoes and sugar to the pan and stir to combine. Return the sausages to the pan and bring to the boil. Reduce the heat to a low simmer and cook for 10–15 minutes. Season to taste with salt and pepper and serve with the side dish of your choice.

Variation: Try using herbed vegetarian sausages and follow the recipe as you would for the pork ones. If you want a bit of spicy heat, add a good pinch of dried chilli flakes or a finely chopped fresh red chilli with the onions.

500 g lamb mince

1 onion, grated

2 garlic cloves, finely chopped

a handful of fresh flat-leaf parsley leaves, finely chopped

2 tablespoons olive oil

1 teaspoon ground cumin

1 teaspoon ground cinnamon

½ teaspoon cayenne pepper

400-g tin chopped tomatoes

a large handful of fresh coriander leaves, finely chopped

Crunchy salad

1 small head of iceberg lettuce, shredded

1 small red onion, very thinly sliced

2 handfuls of fresh mint leaves

2 tablespoons olive oil

1 tablespoon freshly squeezed lemon juice

sea salt and freshly ground black pepper

Serves 4

Put the mince, half of the onion, half of the garlic and the parsley in a bowl. Use your hands to combine and throw the mixture against the side of the bowl several times. Set aside.

Heat the oil in a large heavy-based frying pan set over high heat and cook the remaining onion and garlic for 5 minutes, until softened and golden. Add the spices and cook, stirring constantly, for 1 minute, until aromatic. Add the tomatoes and 250 ml water and bring to the boil. Cook for about 5 minutes.

With slightly wet hands, roll the lamb mixture into walnut-sized balls and put them directly into the sauce mixture as you do so. Reduce the heat, cover with a lid or plate and cook for about 15 minutes, until the meatballs are cooked through. Stir in the coriander and keep warm.

To make the salad, put the lettuce, onion and mint in a salad bowl and toss together. Pour over the olive oil and lemon juice and season to taste with salt and pepper. Serve the kefta with the crunchy salad on the side.

Lamb kefta with crunchy salad

If you are interested in cooking with spices, Moroccan food is a great place to start. This style of cooking uses a relatively short list of staple spices, such as cumin, cinnamon and cayenne pepper, but they are all used in varying quantities to produce very different results from one recipe to the next. These kefta (little meatballs) are made in a large frying pan so this is a great one-pot dish.

Baked chipolatas in tomato and basil sauce on soft polenta

8 good-quality chipolata sausages, pricked with a fork

1 red onion, peeled and cut into thin wedges

4 garlic cloves, roughly chopped

2 tablespoons olive oil

400-g tin chopped tomatoes

a handful of fresh basil leaves

sea salt and freshly ground black pepper

freshly grated Parmesan cheese, to serve

Soft polenta

500 ml full-fat milk

200 g instant polenta

50 g butter, cut into cubes

50 g Parmesan cheese, finely grated

Serves 4

Preheat the oven to 220°C (425°F) Gas 7.

Put the sausages, onion and garlic in a roasting tin and pour over the olive oil. Season well with salt and pepper and cook in the preheated oven for 15 minutes.

Remove the roasting tin from the oven, stir the sausage mixture and pour over the tinned tomatoes. Return to the oven for a further 20 minutes.

Chop some of the basil leaves and stir them into the sausage mixture, reserving a few to garnish.

To make the polenta, put the milk and 500 ml water in a large saucepan and bring to the boil. Pour the polenta into the boiling liquid in a steady stream and whisk constantly, until combined. Reduce the heat to low and beat with a wooden spoon for about 2–3 minutes. Stir in the butter and grated Parmesan.

Spoon the soft polenta onto a large serving platter and top with the sausages and sauce. Sprinkle with the reserved basil leaves and serve immediately with grated Parmesan on the side.

Gnocchetti pasta with smoky chorizo and seared prawns

200 g large raw prawns, peeled and deveined

1 tablespoon red wine vinegar

2 tablespoons olive oil

1 red onion, chopped

1 green pepper, deseeded and thinly sliced

100 g chorizo sausage, finely chopped

½ teaspoon Spanish smoked paprika (pimentón dulce)

400-g tin chopped tomatoes

300 g dried gnocchetti or any other pasta shape, such as fusilli or penne

a handful of fresh mint leaves, chopped

a handful of fresh flat-leaf parsley leaves, roughly chopped

sea salt and freshly ground black pepper

lemon wedges, to serve

Serves 4

Put the prawns in a non-reactive bowl with the vinegar and 1 tablespoon of the olive oil. Season with a little salt and pepper and set aside.

Heat the remaining olive oil in a heavy-based saucepan set over high heat. Add the onion, green pepper and chorizo and cook for 4–5 minutes, until softened and aromatic. Add the paprika and cook for 1 minute, stirring to combine. Add the tomatoes and 125 ml water and bring to the boil. Cook for about 5 minutes, until the sauce has thickened slightly. Set aside while you cook the pasta.

Bring a large saucepan of lightly salted water to the boil. Add the pasta and cook for 12–15 minutes, until tender yet a little firm to the bite. Drain well and return to the warm pan. Add the tomato sauce and keep warm over very low heat while cooking the prawns.

Heat a non-stick frying pan over high heat. Cook the prawns for 2 minutes each side until pink.

Stir the prawns through the pasta and season to taste. Spoon onto serving plates and scatter the mint and parsley over each one. Serve with lemon wedges on the side for squeezing.

Food for friends and family doesn't have to be fussy and formal – most people enjoy a simple dish that's easy to eat yet full of flavour. Simple recipes such as these require few ingredients but they do need to be good quality – always shop well and buy the best you can afford for the tastiest results. Cooking with seasonal produce, fresh herbs and good-quality meat and fish will always create the most memorable meals.

This Moroccan-style fish tagine typifies the simplicity of traditional Moroccan cooking techniques and is full of aromatic spices. Cod, monkfish or any other firm, white fish fillet will work well. Using flavourful, ripe tomatoes will make all the difference, so this is best enjoyed in the summer. Serve with fluffy couscous and a crisp green salad.

Moroccan-style white fish, potato and tomato tagine

5 garlic cloves

1 teaspoon sea salt

2 teaspoons ground cumin

1 teaspoon paprika

1 tablespoon freshly squeezed
lemon juice

a small bunch of fresh coriander,
finely chopped

3 tablespoons olive oil

750 g any firm white fish fillet, such as
cod or monkfish

3 large ripe tomatoes, roughly chopped

8 small waxy potatoes, sliced

a handful of small black olives, stoned

a handful of fresh coriander leaves, to garnish

couscous, to serve

Serves 4

Crush 2 of the garlic cloves and combine them in a large,
non-reactive bowl with the salt, cumin, paprika, lemon juice,
coriander and 1 tablespoon of the oil.

Cut the fish into large chunks and put them in the bowl with
the garlic mixture. Gently toss the fish until it is evenly coated.
Cover and leave to sit at cool room temperature for 1 hour.

Heat the remaining oil in a frying pan set over medium heat
and cook the remaining garlic, finely chopped, for 1 minute. Add
the tomatoes and stir-fry for about 2–3 minutes until softened.

Add the potato slices and 250 ml water. Bring to the boil and
cook for 5 minutes. Add the fish pieces to the pan, reduce the
heat to a low simmer, cover tightly with a lid and cook for about
15 minutes, until the fish is cooked through and the potatoes are
tender. Stir in the olives and season to taste.

Spoon the tagine over couscous and garnish with coriander
leaves to serve.

Keralan prawn curry

*Here is a simple curry that is typical of the dishes
cooked in southern India. Coconuts grow in abundance
there so grated coconut and coconut milk are widely used
in the region's food. Because of the long coastline, lots of
seafood is used too, which means light dishes that require
little cooking – perfect for the stressed midweek cook!*

2 onions, chopped

4 garlic cloves, chopped

2 tablespoons butter

16 large raw prawns, peeled and deveined

2 large fresh green chillies, thinly sliced

4 tomatoes, roughly chopped

2 tablespoons white wine vinegar

5-cm piece of fresh ginger, peeled and cut into matchsticks

60 ml coconut cream

a handful of fresh coriander leaves, chopped

warmed naan breads, to serve

Serves 4

Put the onions and garlic in a food processor and process until
very finely chopped. Set aside.

Heat the butter in a frying pan set over medium heat. When
the butter is sizzling, add the prawns and cook for just 1 minute
on each side, until pale pink and curled. Remove from the pan.

Add the onion mixture and cook for 5 minutes, stirring often,
until softened and golden. Add the chillies, tomatoes, vinegar,
ginger and 125 ml water. Bring to the boil and cook, uncovered,
for 5 minutes, until thickened.

Add the prawns and cook for 2–3 minutes, until they are
cooked through. Stir in the coconut cream and coriander and
gently cook for 1 minute just to heat through.

Serve with warmed naan breads on the side for mopping up
the deliciously creamy sauce.

Thai-style fish with smoky tomato relish

This is an authentic Thai treat you can easily replicate at home. The tasty tomato relish is also great served with grilled chicken or gently heated and stirred through some cooked prawns.

Preheat the oven to 220°C (425°F) Gas 7.

Put the tomatoes, chillies, garlic bulb and shallots in a roasting tin and cook in the preheated oven for 10–15 minutes.

Remove the tin from the oven, transfer the chillies, garlic and shallots to a bowl and cover. (This will make them sweat and therefore be easier to peel.) Return the tomatoes to the oven for a further 5 minutes, then add them to the bowl with the other vegetables and cover.

When cool enough to handle, peel the tomatoes and chillies and put the flesh in a food processor. Squeeze the soft flesh of the shallots and garlic out of their skins and add to the tomato mixture. Blend to make a chunky sauce. Stir in the lemon juice and 1 tablespoon of the fish sauce and set aside.

Reduce the oven temperature to 180°C (350°F) Gas 4. Cut off the coriander roots, clean and roughly chop. Reserve a few leaves to garnish and chop the remaining leaves and stalks. Put the roots in a mortar with the garlic cloves, peppercorns and remaining fish sauce and pound with a pestle to make a paste. Put the fish fillets on the prepared baking tray. Spread a quarter of the coriander paste over each fillet. Cook in the preheated oven for 20 minutes. Serve with the tomato relish spooned over the top and lime halves on the side for squeezing. Garnish with the reserved coriander leaves.

3 ripe tomatoes

2 large fresh red chillies

1 whole garlic bulb, unpeeled

6 shallots, unpeeled

1 tablespoon freshly squeezed lemon juice

2 tablespoons Thai fish sauce

4 long stalks of fresh coriander, with roots intact

4 garlic cloves, chopped

½ teaspoon black peppercorns

4 x 200-g white fish fillets, such as cod, hake, haddock or sea bass

lime halves, for squeezing

a baking tray lined with baking parchment

Serves 4

Za'atar salmon with lentil salad

This blend of thyme, oregano and sesame seeds is called za'atar. Enjoyed all over the Middle East, Morocco and Egypt, it is generally used as a dry condiment to sprinkle on bread dipped in olive oil. This style of cooking is perfect for last-minute entertaining, since with a pinch or two of storecupboard staples you can bring fresh ingredients to life.

65 ml olive oil

2 tablespoons freshly squeezed lemon juice

1 teaspoon dried thyme

1 teaspoon dried wild oregano

1 tablespoon sesame seeds

4 salmon fillets

1 aubergine, cut into small cubes

250 g cherry tomatoes

1 red onion, thinly sliced

2 garlic cloves, chopped

1 teaspoon ground cumin

400-g tin cooked lentils, drained

1 tablespoon red wine vinegar

a large handful of fresh coriander leaves, chopped

sea salt and freshly ground black pepper

a baking tray lined with baking parchment

Serves 4

Preheat the oven to 220°C (425°F) Gas 7.

Put half of the olive oil, lemon juice, thyme, oregano and sesame seeds in a large non-reactive bowl and season with salt and pepper. Whisk with a fork to combine. Add the salmon and toss to coat. Set aside to allow the flavours to develop while you make the salad.

Heat the remaining olive oil in a frying pan set over high heat. Add the aubergine and cook for 2–3 minutes, turning often, until golden. Add the tomatoes, onion and garlic and cook for 2 minutes, shaking the pan so that the tomatoes soften. Add the cumin, lentils and vinegar and remove from the heat. Stir in the chopped coriander.

Put the salmon on the prepared baking tray and cook in the preheated oven for 10 minutes, until just cooked through. Spoon the lentil salad onto a large platter and arrange the salmon on top. Serve immediately.

Seared tuna with tomatoes, rocket and gremolata

This simple dish can equally well be adapted to a conventional grill or a barbecue.*

2 unwaxed lemons

3 large garlic cloves

40 g flat-leaf parsley

2 tablespoons capers, rinsed if salted

6 fresh tuna steaks

350 g good cherry tomatoes, such as pomodorino

100 g wild rocket

sea salt and freshly ground black pepper

extra virgin olive oil, to drizzle

sliced baguette, to serve (optional)

Serves 6

First make the gremolata. Grate the zest finely from the lemons, taking care not to remove too much white pith. Peel the garlic cloves and chop them finely. Take the tough ends off the parsley stalks and finely chop the leaves. Roughly chop the capers, then pull all the ingredients together on the chopping board and chop them together to mix them thoroughly. Set aside in a bowl. Quarter the lemons.

When you're ready to cook, heat a ridged grill pan or frying pan until almost smoking (about 3 minutes). Rub both sides of the tuna steaks with olive oil and season with sea salt rubbed between your fingers and black pepper. Lay as many tuna steaks as you can fit in the pan and cook for about 1½–2 minutes, depending on the thickness and how rare you like them. Turn them over and cook

the other side for 1–1½ minutes. Set aside on a warmed serving dish and cover lightly with foil. Repeat with the remaining tuna steaks.

Rinse the pan under hot running water, dry with kitchen paper and reheat until very hot. Add 2 tablespoons oil and tip in the tomatoes. Cook for 1–1½ minutes, shaking the pan till the skins start to split then turn off the heat. To serve, put a small handful of rocket on each plate, top with a few tomatoes and lay the tuna steaks alongside. Drizzle the tuna and salad with olive oil and a good squeeze of lemon juice, and sprinkle over the gremolata. Serve with slices of crusty baguette, if liked.

*Note: If you use the grill or barbecue to cook the tuna, just sauté the tomatoes quickly in a frying pan to serve with the salad.

Linguine with garlic and chilli clams

1 kg fresh clams, well scrubbed

400 g dried linguine or spaghetti

65 ml extra virgin olive oil

3 garlic cloves, roughly chopped

2 large fresh red chillies, deseeded and chopped

65 ml dry white wine

a handful of fresh flat-leaf parsley leaves, chopped

sea salt and freshly ground black pepper

crusty bread, to serve

Serves 4

You will always see this on the menu at restaurants in Italy, especially in the coastal towns where good seafood is fresh, plentiful and inexpensive. It is one of those restaurant meals you can successfully cook at home in a flash so perfect for entertaining. As always with dishes that have very few ingredients, the quality and freshness of those ingredients is key. Buy your clams as fresh as possible and try to find very small ones – they are sweeter and more tender than the larger varieties. Do use a good, fruity extra virgin olive oil too – you will taste the difference.

Tap each clam lightly on the work surface and discard any that won't close.

Bring a large saucepan of lightly salted water to the boil and cook the pasta for 8–10 minutes, until tender. Return to the warm pan.

Meanwhile, heat the oil in a large saucepan set over medium heat. Add the garlic and chillies and cook until the garlic just starts to sizzle, flavouring the oil without burning. Increase the heat to high,

add the wine and cook until it boils and has reduced by half.

Add the clams, cover the pan tightly and cook for 3–4 minutes, shaking the pan to encourage the clams to open. Discard any clams that don't open.

Add the pasta to the pan, toss to combine and season to taste with salt and pepper. Stir in the parsley and serve immediately with good crusty bread on the side for mopping up the juices.

Linguine with lemon, basil and parmesan cream

This is an easy pasta dish that can be whipped up in no time at all but is sophisticated and indulgent – great for serving to friends at an impromptu midweek gathering. You can add a splash of vodka to the shallots too, which just gives it a slight acidic edge, as wine does. Do make sure you use an unwaxed lemon here.

25 g unsalted butter

2 shallots, finely chopped

1 unwaxed lemon

300 ml whipping cream

200 ml hot chicken or vegetable stock

2 handfuls of basil leaves, plus more to serve

350 g dried linguine or spaghetti

75 g Parmesan or Pecorino shavings, plus extra to serve

sea salt and freshly ground black pepper

Serves 4

Heat the butter in a frying pan and add the shallots. Add a pinch of salt, cover and cook over low heat for 6–7 minutes, stirring occasionally, until soft and glossy.

Put a large saucepan of water on to boil for the pasta. Meanwhile, take a potato peeler and pare off the zest of the lemon, leaving behind the white pith. Try to pare the zest in one long piece so you can easily remove it later.

Add the cream, stock, lemon zest and basil to the shallots and gently simmer for 10–15 minutes, uncovered, until reduced and thickened – it should only just coat the back of a spoon. Cook the linguine in the boiling water until al dente.

Season the sauce with a little salt and lots of black pepper. Remove the lemon zest. Drain the pasta and return it to the pan. Stir in the Parmesan and squeeze in some juice from the lemon. Add more juice or seasoning, to taste. Garnish with basil leaves and Parmesan shavings.

Rosemary risotto with roasted summer vegetables

Fresh, seasonal ingredients are key to the success of this simple risotto; here asparagus, baby courgette, mushrooms and tomatoes have been used. If you want to cook an equally cheap and cheerful version of this risotto in the colder months, try roasting pumpkin, butternut squash or baby carrots until tender and serve them alongside the risotto.

Preheat the oven to 180°C (350°F) Gas 4.

Put 2 tablespoons of the olive oil and the balsamic vinegar in a large bowl and whisk with a fork to combine. Add the tomatoes, courgettes, asparagus and mushrooms and toss to coat. Arrange the vegetables on a baking tray, pour over any liquid from the bowl and cook in the preheated oven for 40 minutes, turning after about 20 minutes. Set aside while cooking the risotto.

Put the stock and wine in a saucepan set over low heat. Put the remaining oil and 1 tablespoon of the butter in a large, heavy-based frying pan and set over medium heat. Cook the onion, garlic and rosemary for 2–3 minutes, until softened. Add the rice and stir for 1 minute until the rice is glossy.

Add about 125 ml of the hot stock to the rice and cook, stirring constantly, until the rice has absorbed almost all the stock. Repeat until all the stock has been used and the rice is tender yet still retains a firmness to the bite. Stir through half of the Parmesan and the remaining butter and season to taste with salt and pepper. Cover, remove from the heat and leave to sit for 5 minutes before serving.

Serve the risotto with the roasted vegetables arranged on the side and the remaining Parmesan sprinkled over the top.

3 tablespoons olive oil

1 tablespoon balsamic vinegar

12 small vine tomatoes

8 baby courgettes, halved lengthways

a bunch of baby asparagus spears, trimmed

12 button mushrooms, stalks removed

1.25 litres vegetable or chicken stock

125 ml dry white wine

2 tablespoons unsalted butter

1 onion, chopped

1 garlic clove, chopped

1 teaspoon finely chopped rosemary needles

330 g risotto rice, such as arborio

100 g Parmesan, finely grated

sea salt and freshly ground black pepper

Serves 4

Home-made potato gnocchi with roasted tomato sauce

Tinned plum tomatoes, when roasted, produce a thick, richly coloured sauce but do try and use the best-quality tinned tomatoes you can find. Gnocchi are surprisingly easy to make and lighter in texture than the type you buy vacuum-packed in supermarkets.

Preheat the oven to 180°C (350°F) Gas 4.

To make the sauce, put the tomatoes and any juice from the tins in a roasting tin with the onions, garlic, sugar and olive oil and sprinkle with a little sea salt. Cook in the preheated oven for 40–45 minutes, stirring after 20 minutes, until thick and deep red in colour. Transfer to a food processor and process until just combined to make a thick, chunky sauce. Set aside until needed.

To make the gnocchi, preheat the oven to 180°C (350°F) Gas 4. Prick the potatoes all over with a fork and put them directly on the middle shelf of the oven. Bake for 1–1½ hours, until the skin is browned and puffed. Remove, cover with a clean tea towel and set aside until cool enough to handle but still warm. The potato flesh needs to be warm for a light textured gnocchi.

Peel and discard the skin from the potatoes, then roughly chop the flesh. Put the chopped potato in a large bowl and mash until smooth (do not use a food processor or the gnocchi will be tough). Mix in the egg yolk, Parmesan and salt. Gradually stir in the flour – you may not need all of it, so add a little at a time until the dough is soft, pliable and damp but not sticky.

Using lightly floured hands, divide the gnocchi dough into 4 portions of equal size. Lightly flour the work surface. Use your hands to roll each portion into a log about 1½ cm in diameter. Using a sharp knife, cut each log into 1½-cm thick discs,

then gently press the back of a fork into each gnocchi to make an indentation.

Bring a large saucepan of lightly salted water to the boil ready to cook the gnocchi. Meanwhile, gently reheat the tomato sauce in a small saucepan set over low heat.

Cook the gnocchi in the boiling water for about 2 minutes, until they have risen to the surface and are tender. Remove from the pan with a slotted spoon, drain well, transfer to serving plates and spoon over the warmed sauce. Serve immediately sprinkled with Parmesan and scatter a few basil leaves over the top.

2 large floury potatoes (about 400 g each), unscrubbed

1 egg yolk

2 tablespoons very finely grated Parmesan

125–150 g plain flour

1 teaspoon sea salt

Parmesan cheese shavings, to serve

a handful of fresh basil leaves, to garnish

Roasted tomato sauce

2 x 400-g tins whole plum tomatoes

2 red onions, chopped

4 garlic cloves, chopped

1 tablespoon soft brown sugar

3 tablespoons olive oil

extra virgin olive oil, to drizzle

sea salt

Serves 4

Pappardelle with roast fennel, tomato and olives

This technique of roasting vegetables in the oven makes easy work of a pasta sauce. The vegetables soften and sweeten while they cook and there is no constant stirring involved as there is with stove-top cooking. If you can't find wide pasta ribbons (pappardelle), simply buy fresh lasagne sheets and cut into strips.

65 ml extra virgin olive oil

4 tomatoes, halved

2 red onions, cut into wedges

4 small courgettes, thickly sliced

2 small fennel bulbs, thickly sliced

2 garlic cloves, thickly sliced

1 teaspoon Spanish smoked paprika (pimentón dulce)

50 g small black olives, stoned

400 g fresh pappardelle

2 tablespoons unsalted butter

salt and freshly ground black pepper

grated Manchego, to serve

Serves 4

Preheat the oven to 220°C (425°F) Gas 7.

Put the olive oil in a roasting tin and put it in the oven for 5 minutes to heat up.

Add all of the vegetables and the garlic to the hot roasting tin and sprinkle over the paprika. Season well with salt and pepper. Roast in the preheated oven for about 20 minutes, giving the tin a shake after 15 minutes. Remove from the oven and stir in the olives. Cover and leave to sit while you cook the pappardelle.

Bring a large saucepan of lightly salted water to the boil. Add the pappardelle and cook according to the packet instructions, or just until the pasta rises to the top – it will cook much quicker than dried pasta. Drain well and return to the warm pan. Add the butter and toss well. Add the roasted vegetables and toss gently to combine everything. Sprinkle with grated Manchego and serve immediately.

Quick chilli meatballs with penne

Here, the filling from sausages is rolled into meatballs and cooked in a spicy tomato sauce. All this takes just 10, maybe 15 minutes, but with delicious results.

2 tablespoons olive oil

1 onion, chopped

2 garlic cloves, crushed

2 x 400-g tins chopped tomatoes

1 tablespoon tomato purée

½ teaspoon sugar

½ teaspoon dried chilli flakes

400 g good-quality beef sausages

400 g dried penne

freshly grated Parmesan, to serve

sea salt and freshly ground black pepper

Serves 4

Heat the oil in a frying pan set over high heat. Add the onion and garlic and cook, stirring, for 2–3 minutes, until softened and starting to turn golden.

Add the tomatoes, tomato purée, sugar, dried chilli flakes and 125 ml water and bring to the boil. Reduce the heat to a simmer.

Using slightly wet hands, squeeze the filling out of the sausage casings and shape it into walnut-sized balls. Add these to the tomato sauce. Simmer the meatballs in the sauce for 5 minutes, shaking the pan often to move the meatballs around so that they cook evenly.

Bring a large saucepan of lightly salted water to the boil and cook the penne for 8–10 minutes, until tender.

Drain the penne well and return it to the warm pan. Season the meatball sauce to taste with salt and pepper. Spoon the penne onto serving plates and top with meatballs and plenty of sauce. Sprinkle with grated Parmesan and serve immediately.

Spring vegetable pasta with lemon

a small bunch of asparagus

150 g shelled fresh peas

a few stalks of sprouting broccoli

150 g shelled broad beans

110 g unsalted butter

1 leek or ½ bunch of spring onions, thinly sliced

284-ml tub double cream

300 g dried egg pasta shapes, such as Campanelle

freshly squeezed juice of 2–3 lemons

3 heaped tablespoons finely chopped fresh parsley

2 heaped tablespoons each finely chopped fresh dill and snipped chives

sea salt and freshly ground black pepper

freshly shaved Parmesan, to serve

Serves 6

This dish is admittedly more vegetable than pasta, but it's one of the most delicious ways to enjoy the new season's produce. You can vary the vegetables depending on what's available. Baby courgettes also work well, as does fennel. The key thing is to cook them until they're only just done to preserve their delicate flavour and bright green colour.

Snap the asparagus spears two-thirds down the stalks and discard the woody ends. Cut the remaining stem into short lengths. Steam them for about 2–3 minutes until just cooked and refresh with cold water. Repeat with the other vegetables, steaming them individually until just cooked. (Pop the broad beans out of their skins for an even sweeter taste.)

Gently melt the butter in a large saucepan or flameproof casserole and cook the leek for a couple of minutes until starting to soften. Tip in the other vegetables, lightly toss with the butter, cover the pan and leave over very low heat, adding the cream once the vegetables have heated through.

Cook the pasta following the instructions on the packet. Reserve a little of the cooking water and drain well. Tip the drained pasta into the vegetables and toss together.

Add the lemon juice and herbs, season with salt and pepper and toss together lightly. Check the seasoning, adding extra salt, pepper, lemon juice or a little of the reserved pasta cooking water to lighten the sauce if you think it needs it. Serve immediately with shavings of Parmesan.

Stuffed giant mushrooms with feta and herbs

This is a great vegetarian recipe that will be appreciated by friends who prefer not to eat meat. The flavour of the nut and feta cheese-stuffed mushrooms is best appreciated if they are left to sit for a short while and served warm rather than piping hot.

8 very large mushrooms, stalks removed

100 g feta cheese, grated

40 g blanched almonds, roughly chopped

50 g stale white breadcrumbs

1 tablespoon chopped fresh flat-leaf parsley

1 tablespoon snipped chives

2 teaspoons olive oil

1 tablespoon chilled butter, finely cubed, plus 2 tablespoons extra

6 baby courgettes, halved lengthways

100 g fine green beans, trimmed

4 small leeks, thinly sliced

65 ml dry white wine

freshly squeezed lemon juice, to taste

sea salt and freshly ground black pepper

an ovenproof baking dish, lightly oiled

Serves 4

Preheat the oven to 170°C (325°F) Gas 3.

Sit the mushrooms, gill-side up, in the prepared baking dish. Put the feta, almonds, breadcrumbs and herbs in a bowl and use your fingers to quickly combine. Stir in the olive oil. Spoon the mixture into the mushrooms and press down gently. Dot the cubed butter over the top. Bake in the preheated oven for about 40–45 minutes, until the mushrooms are soft and the tops golden.

Meanwhile, bring a saucepan of lightly salted water to the boil. Add the courgettes and beans to the water and cook for 1 minute.

Drain well and set aside. About 15 minutes before the mushrooms are cooked, heat the extra 2 tablespoons butter in a frying pan set over high heat. Add the leeks and cook for 2 minutes, stirring until softened. Add the courgettes and beans and cook for about 2–3 minutes, until tender. Add the wine and cook for 1 minute, until almost all of it has evaporated. Add a squeeze of lemon juice and season well.

Arrange the vegetables on a serving plate and sit the stuffed mushrooms on top. Leave to cool slightly before serving.

special occasions

Truffled egg linguine

As well as being fancy, this is great fun – toss it on the plate in front of your guests for a bit of restaurant-style cabaret at home. Try to source some good fresh pasta and quality cheeses for this and taste the difference.

125 ml single cream

1 tablespoon unsalted butter

4 very fresh organic eggs

2 tablespoons olive oil

300 g fresh linguine

1 teaspoon truffle oil

50 g Pecorino, finely grated

50 g Parmesan, finely grated

sea salt

Serves 4

Bring a large saucepan of lightly salted water to the boil. Put the cream and butter in a small saucepan and set over low heat.

Put the olive oil in a large, non-stick frying pan and set over medium heat. Crack one egg at a time into the pan. Alternatively, to help prevent the yolks from breaking, crack each one into a small jug, then pour into the pan. Cook the eggs so that the whites just start to turn and firm up around the edge, then slide them onto a plate.

Cook the pasta in the boiling water for about 2–3 minutes, until it rises to the top – fresh pasta cooks much faster than dried. Working quickly, as you want the pasta to be as hot as possible, drain well and return to the warm pan. Pour in the cream mixture. Gently toss to combine, then divide the pasta between 4 serving plates.

Put an egg on top of each one and drizzle truffle oil over the top. Sprinkle a quarter of the cheeses over each one. Use a spoon and fork to toss all the ingredients together so that the yolk combines with the hot pasta and thickens the sauce, and the egg whites are roughly chopped and combined with the linguine. Eat immediately.

Foraged mushroom risotto

The mushrooms you see for sale will either be cultivated or wild. Wild mushroom varieties are foraged – that is to say, they are hand-picked by experts, enthusiasts and fanatics, called mycologists. They are an exotic treat, and as it is notoriously tricky for the untrained eye to determine safe-to-eat varieties, always buy from a specialist seller.

20 g dried porcini mushrooms

2 tablespoons olive oil

3 tablespoons unsalted butter

500 g mixed wild mushrooms, chopped

1 litre vegetable stock

125 ml dry white wine

1 onion, chopped

2 garlic cloves, finely chopped

330 g risotto rice, such as arborio

100 g Parmesan cheese, finely grated

a handful of fresh flat-leaf parsley leaves, finely chopped

sea salt and freshly ground black pepper

Serves 4

Put the dried mushrooms in a heatproof bowl and pour in 500 ml boiling water. Let soak for 30 minutes, then drain, reserving 250 ml of the liquid. Finely chop the mushrooms and set aside.

Heat 1 tablespoon of the oil and half of the butter in a heavy-based saucepan set over medium heat. Add the fresh mushrooms and cook for 8–10 minutes, stirring often, until softened and aromatic. Remove from the pan and set aside.

Put the reserved mushroom soaking liquid in a separate saucepan. Add the stock and wine and set over low heat.

Add the remaining oil and butter to the mushroom pan. Add the onion and garlic and cook for 2–3 minutes, until softened. Add the rice and stir for 1 minute, until the rice is glossy. Reduce the heat to low, add about 125 ml of the hot stock mixture and cook, stirring often, until the stock has been absorbed. Repeat until all the stock has been used and the rice is tender. Stir in half of the Parmesan and season to taste with salt and pepper. Serve with the chopped parsley and remaining Parmesan sprinkled over the top.

Baked salmon with chilli and fresh herbs

Most of us don't own a fish steamer, but fear not – the trick here is to wrap the salmon in damp newspaper and bake it in the oven. It keeps the fish moist and works perfectly!

1 large salmon fillet (about 700–750 g)

a handful of fresh flat-leaf parsley leaves, chopped

a handful of fresh mint leaves, chopped

2 tablespoons chopped fresh dill

1 large fresh red chilli, thinly sliced

2 spring onions, very thinly sliced on the diagonal

2 tablespoons freshly squeezed lemon juice

3 tablespoons light olive oil

sea salt and freshly ground black pepper

boiled new potatoes, to serve (optional)

Serves 4

Preheat the oven to 220°C (425°F) Gas 7.

Wet some newspaper, enough to cover the base of a roasting tin. Sit a piece of baking parchment on the newspaper and put the fish fillet on the paper. Scatter the chopped herbs, chilli and spring onions over the fish.

Put the lemon juice and olive oil in a small bowl or jug and whisk to combine. Pour over the fish. Season with salt and pepper and lay another sheet of baking parchment loosely on top. Wet some more newspaper and lay it over the roasting tin to cover.

Cook in the preheated oven for about 10 minutes, until the fish is slightly rare in the centre. Remove from the oven, but leave the fish to sit in the paper for 5 minutes to continue steaming. Serve with boiled new potatoes, if liked.

Lobster and chips

Since dealing with a live lobster is possibly not the most relaxing prelude to an evening, buy a cooked one for this luxurious treat.

1 medium cooked lobster

60 g unsalted butter

2 garlic cloves, crushed

2 tablespoons freshly squeezed lime juice

1 teaspoon finely grated fresh ginger

14–16 basil leaves, finely shredded

sea salt and cayenne pepper

hand-cut chips, to serve

a shallow baking dish

lobster crackers or a mallet

Serves 2.

Put the lobster underside downwards on a chopping board and cut through it vertically with a large sharp knife. Carefully extract the white lobster meat from the tail, removing the long, thin membrane near the back. Remove the claws and crack them with lobster crackers or hit them smartly with a mallet. Carefully remove the meat, breaking it up as little as possible. Pick out any remaining white meat from the shell, scrape out the rest and discard. Cut the lobster meat into large chunks. Reserve the empty shells.

Melt the butter gently in a saucepan and stir in the garlic, lime juice and ginger. Add the lobster pieces and warm through for 1–2 minutes without boiling. Add the basil and season with salt and cayenne pepper.

Preheat the grill to high. Carefully transfer the empty lobster shells to a baking dish and reassemble the lobster meat in the shells. Put the dish under the preheated grill for 2–3 minutes until you can hear the lobster meat begin to sizzle. Serve immediately with a few hand-cut chips.

Individual snapper pies

These individual fish pies are very different to the béchamel sauce recipes you may have cooked before. The deliciously rich and sweet onion sauce is based on the French classic 'soubise'. Be ready to give the recipe to your guests!

1 tablespoon olive oil

1 tablespoon unsalted butter

900 g onions, thinly sliced

2 fresh or dried bay leaves

375 ml fish stock

500 ml single cream

1 sheet ready-rolled puff pastry, defrosted if frozen

800 g red snapper fillet, cut into bite-sized pieces

whole milk, for glazing

sea salt and freshly ground black pepper

watercress salad, to serve (optional)

4 individual baking dishes, about 10–15 cm diameter

Serves 4

Heat the olive oil and butter in a heavy-based saucepan set over medium heat. Add the onions and bay leaves and stir well to break up the onions. Cover and cook for about 30 minutes, stirring often so that the onions sweat and soften. Remove the lid and increase the heat to high. Cook for a further 10 minutes, stirring occasionally, so that the onions do not catch and turn a pale caramel colour.

Add the fish stock, bring to the boil and cook until the liquid has reduced by half. Reduce the heat to medium and add the cream. Cook for about 15 minutes, stirring constantly. Remove from the heat and leave to cool. Remove the bay leaves and blend the sauce in a food processor until smooth. Set aside until needed.

Preheat the oven to 220°C (425°F) Gas 7.

Lightly flour a work surface. Roll the pastry out to a thickness of about 2–3 mm. Cut 4 circles from the pastry, using one of the baking dishes as a template.

Spoon half of the onion sauce into each of the baking dishes. Arrange a quarter of the fish pieces on top, then spoon over the remaining sauce. Repeat to fill 4 pies. Cover each pie with a pastry circle and press around the edges with the tines of a fork to seal. Use a sharp knife to make 2–3 small incisions in the pastry to let the steam escape.

Brush the top of each with a little milk to glaze and bake in the preheated oven for about 20–25 minutes, until golden and puffed. Serve with a watercress salad, if liked.

Chicken 'panini' with mozzarella and salsa rossa

This intriguing recipe looks like a classic Italian toasted 'panini' sandwich but is actually a chicken breast, split and stuffed with melting mozzarella, fresh basil and a spicy red pepper and tomato sauce. Simple to prepare yet very impressive.

To make the salsa rossa, grill the pepper until charred all over, then put it in a plastic bag and let cool. Peel and discard the skin, then remove the seeds, reserving any juices. Chop the flesh.

Heat the oil gently in a frying pan, then add the garlic and sauté for 3 minutes. Add the tomatoes, chilli flakes and oregano and simmer gently for 15 minutes. Stir in the chopped pepper and the vinegar and simmer for a further 5 minutes to evaporate any excess liquid. Transfer to a blender and purée until fairly smooth. Add salt and pepper to taste and let cool. (The sauce can be stored in a screw-top jar in the refrigerator for up to 3 days.)

Cut the mozzarella into 8 thick slices and set aside until required.

Put the chicken breasts on a board and, using a sharp knife, cut horizontally through the breast without cutting all the way through. Open out flat and season the insides with a little salt and pepper.

Put 2 basil leaves, a few garlic slices and 2 slices of mozzarella in each breast, then fold back over, pressing firmly together. Secure each one with a cocktail stick.

Brush the parcels with a little oil and cook in a heavy frying pan for about 8 minutes on each side until the chicken is cooked and the cheese is beginning to ooze at the sides.

Serve hot with the salsa rossa, a few extra basil leaves and a lightly dressed baby leaf salad.

250 g mozzarella cheese

4 large boneless, skinless chicken breasts

8 large fresh basil leaves, plus extra, to serve

2 garlic cloves, thinly sliced

1 tablespoon olive oil

sea salt and freshly ground black pepper

Salsa rossa

1 large red pepper

1 tablespoon extra virgin olive oil

2 garlic cloves, crushed

2 large ripe tomatoes, peeled and roughly chopped

a small pinch of dried chilli flakes, crushed

1 tablespoon dried oregano

1 tablespoon red wine vinegar

sea salt and freshly ground black pepper

baby leaf salad, to serve

4 cocktail sticks

Serves 4

Roast ducklings with orange and ginger pilaf

While many of us love duck, most of us would admit to being just a little bit afraid of cooking it at home. But fear not, you can't really go wrong with this recipe! The ducklings are initially slow-cooked, rendering out much of the fat, and then blasted in a hot oven for the remainder of the cooking time, which produces lovely crisp skin. The deliciously spicy orange and ginger rice pilaf makes a perfect accompaniment.

2 ducklings (about 1.5–1.6 kg each)

2 unwaxed oranges

a 10-cm piece of fresh ginger

2 tablespoons olive oil

1 tablespoon unsalted butter

6 shallots, thinly sliced

2 fresh or dried bay leaves

2 garlic cloves, chopped

400 g basmati rice

500 ml chicken stock

a generous pinch of saffron threads

sea salt

watercress, to serve (optional)

a cooking rack and a deep roasting tin

Serves 4

Preheat the oven to 130°C (250°F) Gas ½.

Trim the fatty area around the parson's nose (the tail end of the ducklings). Tuck the neck and wings underneath the bird. Using a skewer, pierce the skin all over without piercing the flesh.

Finely grate the zest of 1 of the oranges and set aside. Cut both oranges in half. Squeeze both oranges to give 125 ml juice. Put 2 of the orange halves in the cavity of each duckling. Thinly slice half of the ginger and put it in with the oranges. Finely grate the remaining ginger and set aside.

Rub the ducklings all over with salt. Sit them on a cooking rack set over a deep roasting tin to collect the rendered fat. Cook in the preheated oven for about 2 hours, basting with the duck fat every 30 minutes or so.

Increase the oven temperature to 220°C (425°F) Gas 7. Pour 250 ml water into the roasting tin. Return the ducklings to the oven and cook for 20–30 minutes more, until the skin is golden and crisp. Remove from the oven and leave to rest for 30 minutes before carving into slices.

Meanwhile, to make the pilaf, heat the oil and butter in a large heavy-based saucepan set over medium heat. Add the orange zest, grated ginger, shallots, bay leaves and garlic and cook, stirring, for 2–3 minutes, until softened.

Add the rice and cook for 2 minutes, stirring to combine the rice with the other ingredients. Add the stock, orange juice and saffron. Briskly stir a few times to remove any stuck-on bits from the bottom of the pan and bring to the boil. Cover and cook over low heat for 20 minutes. Remove from the heat and stir.

To serve, plate a few slices of the duckling with the pilaf on the side and a few sprigs of watercress, if liked.

Turkey breast with olive salsa verde

Lean turkey meat pairs very well with strong flavours, so it works perfectly here with a sharp and tangy salsa. While generally it's better to do plenty of preparation ahead of time when entertaining, here the salsa is definitely best made as close to the time that you intend to eat it as possible. It will oxidize very quickly and lose its vibrant fresh taste.

1 turkey breast, (about 1.8 kg), skin on

2 tablespoons light olive oil

2 teaspoons Spanish smoked paprika (pimentón dulce)

8 slices of prosciutto

sea salt and freshly ground black pepper

Olive salsa verde

100 g green olives, stoned

3 cornichons (baby gherkins)

a large handful each of fresh flat-leaf parsley leaves and mint leaves

2 garlic cloves, chopped

3 anchovy fillets in olive oil, drained

3 tablespoons freshly squeezed lemon juice

125 ml olive oil

new potatoes and sautéed baby carrots, to serve (optional

a large flameproof roasting tin

Serves 6–8

Preheat the oven to 180°C (350°F) Gas 4.

Wash the turkey breast and pat it dry. Season the skin well with salt and pepper. Heat the olive oil in the roasting tin and cook the turkey, skin-side down, for 5 minutes, until the skin is golden. Remove from the tin, leaving any residual oil in the tin. Sprinkle the paprika over the skin. Lay the prosciutto slices side by side and slightly overlapping over the entire skin side of the turkey, tucking them in underneath the breast.

Return the turkey to the roasting tin, sitting it skin-side up. Cook in the preheated oven for 1¼ hours, basting occasionally with the pan juices. Increase the oven temperature to 220°C (425°F) Gas 7 and cook for a further 10–15 minutes, so that the prosciutto and skin become very crisp. Remove from the oven, and lightly cover with kitchen foil.

To make the olive salsa verde, put all of the ingredients in a food processor and process until well combined and coarsely chopped, but do not overprocess.

To serve, carve the turkey into thick slices and plate it up with a few spoonfuls of the olive salsa verde to top. Serve with roast new potatoes and sautéed baby carrots on the side, if liked.

Slow-cooked lamb shanks in red wine with white beans

Lamb shanks have recently became popular again but at one time they were trimmed off and discarded by the butcher. It's great that they are enjoying a revival, as they make easy work of entertaining – you should allow one shank per person, which is simple enough, and the meat is best slow-cooked, which leaves you plenty of time to get on with your other preparations. The addition of white beans makes this a rustic, hearty dish – perfect comfort food for hungry guests.

Put the white beans in a bowl. Cover with cold water and leave to soak for 6 hours or overnight. Drain well and set aside.

Preheat the oven to 170°C (325°F) Gas 3.

Put the lamb shanks in the casserole. Add the pancetta, tomatoes, stock, red wine, sun-dried tomato paste, bay leaf, thyme and half of the parsley. Season well with salt and pepper, stir to combine and cover tightly.

Cook in the preheated oven for 2 hours. Remove the casserole from the oven, turn the shanks over and add the beans. Re-cover and return the casserole to the oven and cook for a further hour, until the mixture is thick and the lamb is very tender.

To serve, spoon a quarter of the beans into each dish, add a lamb shank and spoon some sauce over the top. Sprinkle with the remaining parsley. Serve with some sautéed green beans, if liked.

100 g dried white beans, such as cannellini or butter beans

4 trimmed lamb shanks (about 400 g each)

40 g pancetta, chopped

400-g tin chopped tomatoes

500 ml beef stock

250 ml red wine

2 tablespoons sun-dried tomato paste

1 fresh or dried bay leaf

2 sprigs of fresh thyme

a handful of fresh flat-leaf parsley leaves, finely chopped

sea salt and freshly ground black pepper

sautéed green beans, to serve (optional)

a large casserole

Serves 4

Roast beef rib-eye with café de Paris butter and asparagus

Said to have originated in Geneva in the 1940s, you will see many versions of this delicious butter. Great with steak, but also lovely melted on a piece of fish, hot from the grill. Some recipes have an ingredients list as long as your arm, but essentially it is softened butter combined with curry powder, anchovies, Worcestershire sauce and some fresh green herbs.

To make the café de Paris butter, put all of the ingredients in a food processor and process until well combined. Lay a piece of clingfilm on a work surface. Spoon the butter down the centre, then roll up firmly to make a log. (The butter can be made 1–2 days in advance and refrigerated until needed but should be removed from the refrigerator 1 hour before you plan to serve the beef. It can also be frozen for up to 1 month and defrosted before use.) Remove the beef from the refrigerator 1 hour before cooking and rub it all over with the salt and pepper.

Preheat the oven to 220°C (425°F) Gas 7.

Set the roasting tin over high heat. Add the oil to the pan and heat until very hot. Add the beef and cook for 4 minutes, turning every minute, until it is well browned all over. Transfer the roasting tin to the preheated oven and cook for 10 minutes. Turn the beef over and cook for a further 5 minutes. Remove the beef from the oven and sit it on a large sheet of kitchen foil. Pour over any pan juices and wrap it up in the foil (not too tightly). Let rest in a warm place for 15–20 minutes.

Bring a saucepan of lightly salted water to the boil. Add the asparagus and cook for 1 minute. Drain well. Heat the butter in a frying pan set over high heat. Add the asparagus, season well with salt and pepper and stir-fry for 3–4 minutes, until just wilting and lightly golden.

To serve, plate thick slices of the beef and put a few slices of café de Paris butter on top. Arrange the asparagus alongside.

750–800 g beef rib-eye fillet

1 tablespoon sea salt

½ teaspoon freshly ground black pepper

1 tablespoon olive oil

a bunch of white asparagus, trimmed and halved

a bunch of green asparagus, trimmed and halved

2 tablespoons butter

Café de Paris butter

1 tablespoon mild mustard

2 teaspoons Worcestershire sauce

3 tablespoons tomato purée

1 teaspoon mild curry powder

1 tablespoon finely chopped shallots

1 garlic clove, crushed

1 tablespoon salted capers, rinsed, well drained and chopped

6 anchovy fillets in olive oil, drained and finely chopped

2 tablespoons chopped fresh parsley

1 teaspoon fresh thyme leaves

115 g unsalted butter, softened

a large, flameproof roasting tin

Serves 4

feeding a crowd

Soft goats' cheese and fennel tart

The idea of making your own pastry can be a little daunting. That said, this pastry recipe is so unintimidating that you should give it a go. It has just two ingredients and there is no rolling! Make the pastry in the food processor, form it into a ball, then press it directly into the tart tin with your hands. The whole tart can be made well in advance and served at room temperature with a peppery wild rocket salad. It's perfect for a casual weekend lunch or as the vegetarian option in a buffet.

4 fennel bulbs, with feathery tops intact

2 tablespoons olive oil

200 g soft goats' cheese, roughly crumbled

65 g walnut halves

3 eggs

185 ml single cream

1 tablespoon snipped chives

sea salt and freshly ground black pepper

wild rocket, to serve

No-roll pastry

170 g plain flour

80 g unsalted butter, cut into cubes and chilled

a 24-cm loose-bottomed tart tin, lightly greased

baking weights (optional)

Serves 6–8

Preheat the oven to 180°C (350°F) Gas 4.

To make the pastry, put the flour in a food processor. With the motor running, add the butter and process until the mixture resembles coarse breadcrumbs. Add 2–3 tablespoons chilled water and process until the dough just starts to come together. Tip the dough out onto a lightly-floured work surface and use your hands to form it into a ball, gathering all the smaller pieces together. Do not knead it too much.

Put the dough in the centre of the prepared tart tin and use your thumbs to press it down into the tin, working outwards from the centre and making sure the pastry comes up over the side of the tin. Prick the base all over with the tines of a fork. Cover the pastry with a sheet of baking parchment and fill with baking weights, dried beans or rice. Bake in the preheated oven for about 20 minutes, until the pastry looks dry and golden.

Remove the feathery tops from the fennel. Chop them finely to give about 3 tablespoons and set aside. Cut the fennel bulbs into thin wedges. Put them in a roasting tin, add the olive oil and season well with salt and pepper. Cook in the still-hot oven for 40 minutes, turning after 20 minutes, until golden and tender. Leave to cool to room temperature.

Arrange the fennel in the tart case and scatter the cheese and walnuts randomly over and in between the pieces of fennel.

Put the eggs, cream and chives in a jug or bowl. Whisk with a fork to combine, season well and pour over the fennel. Bake in the still-hot oven for about 45 minutes, until puffed and golden on top. Serve the tart at room temperature with a lightly dressed wild rocket salad on the side.

Peel and roughly chop the potatoes. Put them in a large saucepan of lightly salted boiling water and boil for 12–15 minutes, until tender but not falling apart. Drain well, return to the warm pan and roughly mash. Add the milk and nutmeg and season to taste with salt and pepper. Beat with a large wooden spoon or hand-held electric whisk until smooth. Stir through half of the butter, until well combined. Spoon about one-third of the mixture into the baking dish.

Preheat the oven to 180°C (350°F) Gas 4.

Heat half of the remaining butter in a large frying pan set over medium heat. Add the mushrooms, garlic and spring onions and gently fry for 10 minutes or until golden. Spoon over the potato mixture in the baking dish.

Heat the remaining butter in the frying pan and cook the spinach for 5 minutes, stirring often, until just wilted and tender. Season to taste and spoon over the mushroom mixture in the baking dish.

Spoon the remaining mashed potatoes on top of the spinach and scatter over the cubed fontina. Bake in the preheated oven for about 30 minutes, until the cheese is bubbly and golden. Serve warm.

Variation: Swiss chard could be used instead of the spinach, making sure the tough stalks have been removed. You could also try adding 200 g sliced, chargrilled artichoke hearts, available from most delis and supermarkets, and add these after the mushrooms have been cooked off.

Mushroom, spinach and potato bake

This is hearty, comforting and tasty, and will satisfy the hungriest of guests. It uses relatively inexpensive ingredients, so is a great option if you are on a budget. Fontina is a dense, nutty Italian cheese that melts beautifully and gives the mashed potatoes a delicious golden crust. It can be baked in and served from the same dish, which makes light work of the clearing up after your guests have gone.

1 kg floury potatoes

125 ml whole milk

a pinch of freshly grated nutmeg

125 g unsalted butter, cut into cubes

500 g small chestnut mushrooms, left whole and stalks removed

4 garlic cloves, roughly chopped

4 spring onions, cut into 2-cm lengths

1 kg fresh spinach leaves, well washed and roughly chopped

200 g fontina cheese, cut into cubes

sea salt and freshly ground black pepper

a large lasagne dish, or similar

Serves 6

Heirloom tomato, pepper and mozzarella tart

375-g sheet of ready-rolled puff pastry, thawed if frozen

1 large red pepper

1 large yellow pepper

3 tablespoons olive oil

2 garlic cloves, unpeeled and flattened

4 heaped tablespoons fresh red pesto

150 g buffalo mozzarella, thinly sliced

125 g red cherry tomatoes, halved

125 g yellow cherry tomatoes, halved

½ teaspoon dried oregano or marjoram

1 egg, lightly beaten

25 g Parmesan, shaved

a few fresh basil leaves, torn

sea salt and freshly ground black pepper

a roasting tin

a rectangular baking tray, lightly greased

Serves 6–8

There are so many beautifully coloured tomatoes and peppers available no to make this spectacular-looking tart, full of fresh Mediterranean flavours.

Preheat the oven to 200°C (400°F) Gas 6.

Take the pastry out of the fridge at least 20 minutes before you need to unroll it. Quarter the peppers, remove the pith and seeds and cut each quarter into half lengthways. Put them in a roasting tin with the garlic cloves, pour over 2 tablespoons of the oil and mix together well. Roast for about 20–25 minutes until the edges of the peppers are beginning to blacken. Remove and leave to cool for 10 minutes.

Unroll the pastry and lay on the baking tray. Using a sharp knife, score a line around the pastry about 1¼ cm from the edge. Spread the pesto evenly inside the rectangle you've marked. Lay the pepper strips across the base of the tart, alternating red and yellow sections. Distribute the mozzarella pieces over the peppers. Season generously with black pepper. Arrange the halved tomatoes over the peppers, red on yellow and yellow on red. Sprinkle the oregano over the tart, season with a little salt and a little more pepper and trickle over the remaining oil.

Increase the oven temperature to 220°C (425°F) Gas 7. Brush the edges of the tart with the egg and bake for 12 minutes or until the edge of the tart is well puffed up and beginning to brown. Turn the heat back down again to 200°C (400°F) Gas 6 and cook for another 12–15 minutes until the tops of the tomatoes are well browned. Scatter the Parmesan shavings over the tart, then leave to cool for 5 minutes. Scatter the basil over the tart to finish. Serve warm.

Fresh mussels with fennel aïoli

Although you can buy ready-cooked and flavoured vacuum-packed mussels, it's so much better from both a cost and a flavour point of view to buy them really fresh and clean them yourself. Most of their sold weight is shell, but when cooked in a tasty broth and served with bread on the side they are surprisingly filling, and made for sharing. Eating them always creates a lot of mess, but that's all part of the fun!

1 kg fresh mussels

2 small fennel bulbs, with feathery tops intact and reserved for aïoli

1 tablespoon olive oil

1 tablespoon unsalted butter

1 garlic clove, finely chopped

2 shallots, finely chopped

125 ml dry white wine

250 ml fish stock

2 ripe tomatoes, diced

a handful of fresh flat-leaf parsley, roughly chopped

2 baguettes, to serve

Fennel aïoli

reserved fennel tops (see above)

185 ml mayonnaise

3 garlic cloves, crushed

Serves 4

Scrub the mussels well, knock off any barnacles and pull off the beards. Discard any broken mussels and any that won't close when they are tapped on the work surface. Drain in a colander and set aside until needed.

To make the aioli, finely chop the feathery tops of the fennel and combine in a small bowl with the mayonnaise and garlic. Cover with clingfilm and chill until needed.

Finely chop the fennel bulbs. Heat the olive oil and butter in a large stockpot or saucepan set over medium heat and gently cook the garlic, shallots and fennel for about 10 minutes, until the fennel has softened.

Add the white wine, stock and tomatoes and bring to the boil. Cook for 5 minutes. Add the mussels, cover tightly with a lid and cook for a further 5 minutes, shaking the pan occasionally, until the mussels have opened. Discard any that don't open. Add the parsley and stir.

Spoon the mussels into deep serving bowls and put a large, empty bowl on the table for discarded shells. Offer the fennel aïoli on the side for spooning and serve with warmed baguette.

Variation: For a tasty alternative, try adding 1 finely diced chorizo sausage to the pan when cooking off the garlic, shallots and fennel.

Shepherd's pie

Old-school, traditional fare like shepherd's pie never goes out of style. If you want to make this a little smarter, you can bake it in individual ovenproof dishes, but to keep it casual simply put the dish in the centre of the table and let everyone help themselves.

2 tablespoons olive oil

125 g unsalted butter

2 large onions, chopped

2 carrots, grated

2 celery sticks, chopped

750 g lamb mince

1 litre beef stock

2½ tablespoons cornflour

a large handful of fresh flat-leaf parsley leaves, finely chopped

1 kg floury potatoes, peeled and quartered or halved, depending on size

85 ml whole milk

sea salt and freshly ground black pepper

a large ovenproof baking dish

Serves 6

Heat the oil and 1 tablespoon of the butter in a large, heavy-based frying pan set over high heat. When the butter has melted and is sizzling, add the onions and cook for 5 minutes, until golden. Add the carrots and celery and cook for a further 5 minutes. Add the mince and cook for about 10 minutes, until it has browned, stirring often to break up any large clumps.

Put the cornflour in a small bowl and stir in 65 ml of the stock. Add the remaining stock to the pan with the mince and cook for 10 minutes, letting the stock boil and reduce a little.

Add the cornflour mixture to the pan and cook, stirring constantly, until the liquid thickens to a gravy. Stir in the parsley, season well with salt and pepper and set aside. Preheat the oven to 180°C (350°F) Gas 4.

Put the potatoes in a large saucepan of lightly salted boiling water. Cook for 10 minutes, until they are just starting to break up and the water is cloudy. Drain well and return to the warm pan. Add the remaining butter and the milk and season to taste with salt and pepper. Roughly mash to leave the potatoes with a chunky texture.

Spoon the mince into the baking dish and spread the mashed potatoes over the top. Cook in the preheated oven for 40–45 minutes, until the potato is crisp and golden brown.

Variation: You could also use beef or pork mince as an alternative to the lamb. Try adding some thinly sliced leeks or finely chopped fennel bulbs when you are cooking the onions.

Shoulder of lamb with oven-roasted vegetables

A shoulder of lamb is generally a cheaper cut than others all year round, but slow-cooked in this way it's truly delicious and guaranteed to satisfy the hungriest of guests. Rather than cooking potatoes and vegetables separately, as is traditional, here they are roasted alongside the meat and make a very tasty accompaniment.

1.5 kg shoulder of lamb, on the bone

500 ml dry white wine

250 ml freshly squeezed lemon juice

3 tablespoons olive oil

4 sprigs of fresh rosemary

2 teaspoons dried oregano, preferably Greek

4 garlic cloves, lightly smashed

1 large courgette, roughly chopped

1 large red onion, peeled and cut into thin wedges

1 small yellow pepper, deseeded and thickly sliced

3 waxy potatoes, thickly sliced

1 tablespoon finely chopped fresh dill

a handful of fresh flat-leaf parsley leaves, roughly chopped

sea salt and freshly ground black pepper

a large flameproof roasting tin

kitchen string

Serves 6

Put the lamb, skin-side up, in a non-reactive dish. Add the wine, lemon juice, 2 tablespoons of the olive oil, the rosemary, oregano and garlic. Cover and refrigerate overnight.

Remove from the refrigerator 1 hour before cooking and season the skin of the lamb well with salt and pepper.

Preheat the oven to 220°C (425°F) Gas 7.

Remove the lamb from the marinade, reserving 2 tablespoons of the liquid. Roll it firmly and secure with kitchen string.

Put the courgette, onion, pepper and potatoes in a bowl with the reserved marinade and use your hands to toss the vegetables until coated.

Set a roasting tin over high heat and add the remaining olive oil. Heat until very hot. Add the lamb and cook for 5–6 minutes, turning often, until golden all over. Add the vegetables to the tin and cook for 2–3 minutes, turning the vegetables often. Transfer to the preheated oven and cook for 40 minutes, turning the vegetables after 20 minutes. Transfer the vegetables to a bowl, cover with kitchen foil and keep warm.

Reduce the oven temperature to 180°C (350°F) Gas 4. Cook the lamb for a further hour, until the skin is dark and crisp. Remove from the oven and cover tightly with kitchen foil. Leave to rest in a warm place for about 20 minutes before carving.

Add the dill and parsley to the warm vegetables and season to taste with salt and pepper.

To serve, plate thick slices of the lamb with the vegetables on the side.

Chicken, lemon and green olive tagine

A fabulously fragrant chicken casserole that can be easily made ahead of time and reheated just before serving.

Remove any excess fat from the chicken thighs and cut them in half. Heat the oil in the casserole, add the sliced onions and garlic and cook over medium heat for 7–8 minutes until the onions have started to soften and collapse.

Add the chicken thighs, mix well with the onions and continue to cook for about 10 minutes over low heat, stirring occasionally. Put the saffron in a mortar and crush with a pestle. Pour over about 2 tablespoons of the stock and leave for a few minutes to infuse. Stir the saffron and ginger into the chicken. Quarter the preserved lemons, scoop out the flesh and finely sliced the peel. Add the olives and preserved lemon to the chicken. Pour in the remaining stock and mix well.

Thoroughly wash the coriander, cut off the stalks, tie them together with a piece of cotton or string and lay them in the casserole. Put a lid on the pan and leave to simmer until the chicken is cooked (about another 30 minutes). Remove the coriander stalks and season the tagine to taste with lemon juice, salt and pepper.

Put the harissa paste, if using, into a bowl, spoon off about 4–5 tablespoons of the liquid from the tagine and mix with the harissa. Roughly chop the coriander leaves, stir into the tagine and serve the harissa on the side for those that want it. Serve with some sautéed green beans, if liked.

12 skinless, boneless chicken thighs
(about 1 kg in total)

3 tablespoons olive oil

400 g onions, sliced

2 garlic cloves, crushed

a good pinch of saffron threads

300 ml chicken or light vegetable stock

1 teaspoon finely grated fresh ginger or
½ teaspoon ground ginger

2 small preserved lemons

75 g stoned green olives (ideally marinated with herbs)

a small bunch of fresh coriander

1–2 tablespoons freshly squeezed lemon juice

sea salt and freshly ground black pepper

1 teaspoon harissa paste, to serve (optional)

sautéed green beans, to serve (optional)

a large flameproof casserole

Serves 6

Beef daube

This is definitely not fast food, so relax and let the ingredients and your oven do all the work. You can use a cheaper cut of meat here and it will still taste good after a long marinating and cooking time.

750 g chuck steak, in one large piece

1 large carrot, diced

1 celery stick, diced

1 fresh or dried bay leaf

3 garlic cloves, unpeeled and smashed

500 ml red wine

1 tablespoon olive oil

1 tablespoon butter, plus extra for the peas

400-g tin chopped tomatoes

250 ml beef stock

400 g dried pasta tubes, such as rigatoni

130 g frozen baby peas

50 g Parmesan cheese, finely grated

sea salt and freshly ground black pepper

a large flameproof casserole

Serves 6–8

Put the beef in a non-reactive dish with the carrot, celery, bay leaf, garlic and red wine. Cover and refrigerate overnight, turning occasionally. Set a colander over a large bowl and tip the entire contents of the dish into it. Remove the meat and leave the vegetables in the colander to drain. Reserve the marinating liquid.

Heat the oil and butter in the casserole over medium/high heat. Add the beef and cook for 8 minutes, turning every 2 minutes, until very dark. Remove from the casserole. Add the carrot, celery, bay leaf and garlic to the pan and cook for 5 minutes, until the carrot is tender. Add the reserved marinating liquid and cook for about 8–10 minutes, until the liquid has reduced by half and become aromatic.

Return the beef to the casserole with the tomatoes and stock. Bring to the boil, then reduce the heat to a gentle simmer. Partially cover and cook for 1 hour, until the meat is tender. Remove the meat from the pan and roughly shred it with a fork. Boil the sauce for 10 minutes, until thickened. Return the meat to the casserole and season to taste with salt and pepper. Keep warm until ready to serve.

Cook the pasta according to the packet instructions. Drain and return it to the warm saucepan. Cook the peas until tender. Drain and return to the warm saucepan with 1 tablespoon butter, stirring until it has melted. Combine the beef and pasta and serve with the peas spooned over the top and a sprinkle of grated Parmesan.

Slow-cooked spiced pork belly with apples and fennel

This recipe uses pork belly, but you could roast a shoulder or leg joint of pork if preferred. You can't go far wrong with this low-temperature, slow-cooking method, which produces crispy skin and melt-in-the-mouth meat. It will greet your guests with a delicious aroma, creating a mood of anticipation, which is one of the keys to successful entertaining.

1 tablespoon fennel seeds

2 teaspoons caraway seeds

4 garlic cloves

2 tablespoons olive oil

1 kg pork belly

4 apples, such as Cox's Orange Pippin

2 fennel bulbs, with feathery tops intact, cut into thick wedges

sea salt and freshly ground black pepper

Serves 6

Combine the fennel and caraway seeds, garlic and 1 tablespoon salt in a mortar and pound with a pestle. Stir in half of the olive oil.

Cut ½-cm deep incisions, spaced 1–2 cm apart, across the skin of the pork. Rub the spice mixture into the incisions, and let sit for 1 hour at cool room temperature.

Preheat the oven to 140°C (275°F) Gas 1.

Put the pork in a large roasting tin and cook in the preheated oven for 3 hours in total. (You'll remove the tin from the oven 30 minutes before the end of the cooking time to add the apples and fennel.)

Put the remaining oil in a large bowl and season with a little salt and pepper. Add the apples and the fennel bulbs with feathery tops to the bowl and use your hands to toss until evenly coated in oil.

Thirty minutes before the end of the cooking time, remove the pork from the oven and arrange the apples and fennel in the tin. Increase the oven temperature to 220°C (425°F) Gas 7 and return the tin to the oven.

Remove the pork from the oven, cover loosely with kitchen foil and leave to rest for about 20 minutes.

To serve, carve into slices and plate with the roasted apples and fennel on the side.

Brined roast chicken with a ham and fresh sage stuffing

Brining is the most basic of marinades. Prepared and cooked this way, your roast chicken will be full of flavour and truly memorable. If you are pressed for time, you can leave out the brining, but I strongly recommend that you don't. If you are brining, do bear in mind that the chicken will need to be in the liquid for at least three hours and removed from the brine one hour before cooking.

3 tablespoons sea salt

2 tablespoons white sugar

2 fresh or dried bay leaves

1 roasting chicken, about 1.8 kg

2 tablespoons butter, softened

Ham and fresh sage stuffing

5 slices of stale white bread, crusts removed, roughly torn

2 tablespoons butter

1 small onion, finely chopped

2 garlic cloves, chopped

100 g smoked ham, finely chopped

2 tablespoons finely chopped fresh sage

1 egg

a large non-reactive bowl or bucket, big enough to take the chicken and 3 litres liquid

kitchen string

Serves 4

Put the salt, sugar and bay leaves in a very large saucepan with 3 litres water. Bring to the boil, stirring a few times until the salt and sugar have dissolved, then remove from the heat. Leave to cool to room temperature. Sit the chicken in the non-reactive bowl and pour in the liquid so that the chicken is fully immersed. Cover and put somewhere cold to sit for 3–6 hours.

To make the stuffing, put the bread in a food processor and process to make coarse crumbs. Tip the crumbs into a bowl and set aside.

Heat the butter in a saucepan set over medium heat and cook the onion for 5 minutes, until softened. Add the garlic, ham and sage and stir-fry for 1 minute. Add the mixture to the crumbs with the egg and use your hands to combine well.

Remove the chicken from the brine 1 hour before cooking. Preheat the oven to 170°C (325°F) Gas 3.

Spoon the stuffing into the cavity of the chicken and tie the legs firmly together with kitchen string.

Put the chicken in a roasting tin and rub the butter over the top side. Roast in the preheated oven for 1½ hours, until the skin of the chicken is golden and the meat is cooked through. To test, insert a skewer into the chicken where the leg joins the breast; if the juices run clear, it is cooked. Let the chicken rest in a warm place for 30 minutes before carving.

To serve, carve and plate with sautéed potatoes and a side vegetable of your choice, such as green beans.

Vietnamese chicken curry

The inclusion of both bay leaves and lemongrass here may seem a little odd, but Vietnamese cuisine has been strongly influenced by French cooking styles. Curries in Vietnam are served in a large bowl placed in the centre of the table, along with crusty baguettes instead of the more traditional rice.

1 chicken, about 1.8 kg, cut into 10–12 pieces

2 tablespoons mild curry powder

3 tablespoons light olive oil

2 onions, cut into thick wedges

3 garlic cloves, roughly chopped

1 lemongrass stalk, gently bruised

3 dried or fresh bay leaves

2 carrots, cut into thick chunks

2 x 400-ml tins coconut milk

½ teaspoon caster sugar

sea salt and freshly ground black pepper

1–2 baguettes, to serve

a flameproof casserole (optional)

Serves 4

Put the chicken pieces in a large bowl. Add the curry powder, 1 teaspoon sea salt and some black pepper. Use your hands to toss the chicken until it is evenly coated in the curry mixture.

Put 1 tablespoon of the oil in a casserole or large, heavy-based saucepan and set over medium heat. Add half of the chicken pieces and cook for 5 minutes, turning often, until golden brown and crisp. Transfer to a plate.

Add another tablespoon of oil to the pan and cook the remaining chicken pieces in the same way. Add them to the first batch. Pour the remaining oil into the pan and add the onions, garlic and lemongrass. Cook for 5 minutes, until the onions are golden and soft, stirring occasionally.

Add the bay leaves and carrots to the pan and cook for about 2–3 minutes. Increase the heat to high. Add the coconut milk and sugar and bring to the boil, stirring often. Reduce the heat to medium. Cook for 10 minutes. Add all the chicken pieces, except any from the breast, and cook for 10 minutes. The liquid should be gently simmering, not boiling. Add the remaining chicken and any collected juices and cook for a further 10 minutes, until the chicken is cooked through. Serve with plenty of fresh baguette for mopping up the sauce.

Coq au leftover red wine with garlic mash

Although any leftover red wine will do for this recipe, pinot noir works very well. It may not be that cheap but if you have genuine leftovers that are no longer drinkable, it's better to put them to good use than to waste them. Using chicken drumsticks in recipes that typically call for a whole bird to be cut into portions not only saves you time but you can more easily calculate portion size and double this recipe for a larger crowd. Bear in mind that the chicken marinates in the wine overnight, so you'll need to start prepping the day before you intend to serve. A fluffy garlic mash makes the perfect accompaniment.

8 chicken drumsticks

250 ml pinot noir or any other red wine

1 onion, chopped

1 carrot, diced

1 celery stick, diced

4 garlic cloves, sliced

1 dried or fresh bay leaf

4 tablespoons olive oil

12 pickling onions or small shallots

4 bacon rashers, roughly chopped

100 g button mushrooms, stalks removed

500 ml beef stock

sea salt and freshly ground black pepper

Garlic mash

800 g floury potatoes, peeled and quartered or halved, depending on size

125 ml whole milk

3 garlic cloves, crushed

75 g butter

a large flameproof casserole (optional)

Serves 4

Put the chicken drumsticks in a non-reactive dish with the red wine, onion, carrot, celery, garlic and bay leaf. Cover and refrigerate overnight, turning the chicken occasionally.

Set a colander over a large bowl and tip the entire contents of the dish into it. Transfer the chicken drumsticks to a plate and leave the vegetables in the colander to drain. Reserve the marinating liquid.

Heat 1 tablespoon of the oil in a casserole or large, heavy-based saucepan and cook the pickling onions and bacon for 4–5 minutes, shaking the pan often, until golden. Remove from the pan and set aside. Add another tablespoon of the oil to the pan and cook the mushrooms for 5 minutes, until golden and softened. Remove from the pan and set aside.

Add another tablespoon of the oil to the pan and cook half of the chicken drumsticks for a few minutes until well browned all over. Transfer to a plate. Add the remaining oil and chicken to the pan and repeat. Add the drained vegetables, garlic and bay leaf to the pan and cook for 5 minutes, until softened and golden.

Return the chicken, pickling onions and bacon to the pan along with the reserved marinating liquid and the beef stock. Bring to the boil, then reduce the heat to medium, cover and cook for about 20 minutes, until the chicken is cooked

through and tender. Add the mushrooms and cook for another 5 minutes.

Meanwhile, make the garlic mash. Cook the potatoes in a large saucepan of lightly salted boiling water for 15 minutes, until very tender. Drain well and return to the warm pan. Put the milk, garlic and butter in a small saucepan and cook over low heat until the butter has melted. Add the milk mixture to the potatoes and mash or ideally beat with a hand-held electric mixer until smooth and fluffy. Season to taste with salt and pepper.

To serve, put 2 drumsticks per person onto plates and spoon over the sauce and vegetables. Put a large scoopful of the garlic mash on the side.

Boeuf bourguignon with pomme purée

900 g braising beef or steak

3 tablespoons olive oil

130 g cubed pancetta

3 onions, finely chopped

2 large garlic cloves, finely chopped

1½ tablespoons plain flour

450 ml red wine, plus an extra splash if needed

a bouquet garni made from a few sprigs of thyme, parsley stalks and a bay leaf

25 g unsalted butter

250 g chestnut mushrooms, cleaned and halved

2 tablespoons finely chopped fresh flat-leaf parsley

salt and freshly ground black pepper

Pomme purée

1 kg red-skinned potatoes, such as Desirée or Wilja

50 ml double cream

75–100 ml whole milk

75 g unsalted butter, cut into cubes and at room temperature

sea salt and freshly ground black pepper

a large flameproof casserole

a potato ricer

Serves 6

Although Boeuf Bourguignon sounds as if it should be made with red Burgundy, it is actually tastier made with a fuller-bodied red wine, such as one from the Rhône or Languedoc. If possible, make it a day ahead to allow the flavours to develop but it's not essential to do so. Pomme purée is the decadent French way of cooking mash and well worth the extra effort involved for a velvety smooth treat.

Pat the meat dry, trim off any excess fat or sinew and cut into large chunks. Heat 1 tablespoon of the oil in a large frying pan and sauté the pancetta until lightly browned. Remove from the pan with a slotted spoon and transfer to a flameproof casserole. Brown the meat in 2 batches in the fat that remains in the frying pan and add to the bacon. Add the remaining oil to the frying pan and fry the onion slowly until soft and caramelized (about 25 minutes), adding the chopped garlic halfway through the cooking time. Stir the flour into the onions, cook for a minute, then add the wine and bring to the boil. Pour over the meat, add the bouquet garni and bring back to the boil. Turn down the heat and simmer over very low heat for 2–2½ hours, until the meat is just tender. Turn off the heat, cover the casserole with the lid and leave overnight.

The next day, bring the casserole back to boiling point, then turn down low again. Heat the butter in a frying pan and fry the mushrooms until lightly browned (about 5 minutes). Tip the mushrooms into the stew, stir and cook for about 10–15 minutes. Season the casserole to taste with salt and pepper, adding an extra splash of wine if the flavour is not quite pronounced enough.

To make the pomme purée, peel the potatoes and cut them into quarters or eighths (about half the size you would cut them for normal mash). Put them in a saucepan, pour over boiling water, add 1 teaspoon salt and bring back to the boil. Turn down the heat and simmer gently for about 12–15 minutes until you can easily pierce them with a skewer. Drain them in a colander, then return them to the pan over very low heat and leave them for 1–2 minutes to dry off.

Mix the cream and milk together and heat until just below boiling point in a microwave or separate saucepan.

Tip the potatoes back into the colander, then pass them through a potato ricer back into the pan. Pour in half the cream mixture and beat with a wooden spoon, then gradually beat in the remaining cream mixture and the butter. Season to taste with salt and pepper.

To serve, spoon the boeuf bourguignon onto plates and scatter over the chopped parsley. Add a scoopful of pomme purée on the side.

desserts
and cheese

An affogato is a fantastic Italian dessert – a scoop of vanilla ice cream is doused in a shot of hot espresso coffee and sometimes a sweet Italian liqueur such as Frangelico, Amaretto or Strega. Here we have all the flavours of an affogato in a parfait log. You can make it in advance, then simply remove it from the freezer, sprinkle with nuts, slice and serve with a little glass of liqueur on the side, if liked.

Affogato parfait

125 ml hot strong black
espresso coffee

125 g caster sugar

1 vanilla pod

5 egg yolks

3 tablespoons Frangelico (Italian
hazelnut liqueur) or grappa

500 ml crème fraîche

250 ml double cream

100 g hazelnuts, lightly toasted
and roughly chopped

*a loaf tin, 8 x 22 cm, lined
with clingfilm*

Serves 6–8

Put the coffee and sugar in a small saucepan and set over high
heat. Rub the vanilla pod between your palms to soften it, then
use a sharp knife to split it open lengthways. Scrape the seeds
directly into the saucepan. Bring the mixture to the boil, then
reduce the heat to medium and leave the liquid to simmer for
about 10 minutes, stirring occasionally, until syrupy. Remove from
the heat.

Put the egg yolks in a large bowl and use a balloon whisk to
beat until thick and pale. Add the warm coffee syrup. Beat until
well combined, then add the Frangelico. Add the crème fraîche
and cream and beat until well combined. Pour into the prepared
loaf tin and freeze overnight.

Remove the parfait from the freezer and let it sit for a few
minutes before carefully turning out onto a chilled serving platter.
Sprinkle with the hazelnuts and slice with a hot knife to serve.

Variation: For an almond-flavoured version, use Amaretto
di Saronno instead of Frangelico and sprinkle the parfait with
toasted flaked almonds or crushed amaretti biscuits.

Sparkling Shiraz and summer berry jellies

9 sheets of gelatine (or enough to
set 750 ml of liquid)

750 ml sparkling Shiraz or other
sparkling red wine

600 g mixed fresh red berries,
such as strawberries, raspberries,
blackberries, blueberries,
blackcurrants or redcurrants

2–3 tablespoons caster sugar,

depending on how ripe your
berries are

6–8 tablespoons home-made sugar
syrup* or shop-bought gomme

*8 glasses or small glass
serving dishes*

Serves 8

Put the gelatine in a flat dish and sprinkle over 4 tablespoons
cold water. Leave to soak for 3 minutes until soft. Heat the wine
in a microwave or saucepan until hot but not boiling. Tip the
gelatine into the wine and stir to dissolve, then set aside to cool.
Rinse the berries, cut the strawberries into halves or quarters,
then put them in a shallow bowl, sprinkle over the sugar and
leave them to macerate. Check the liquid jelly for sweetness,
adding sugar syrup to taste.

Put an assortment of berries in the glasses, then pour over
enough jelly to cover them. Put in the fridge to chill. As soon as
the jelly has set (about 1 hour) add the rest of the fruit and jelly.
Return the jellies to the fridge to set for another 45–60 minutes
before serving.

* To make the sugar syrup, dissolve 125 g sugar in 150 ml
water. Heat gently together in a pan. When all the grains are
dissolved, bring to the boil and simmer for 2–3 minutes. Use it
immediately or cool and store it for up to two weeks in the fridge.

Chocolate marquise

If you are a fan of real chocolate mousse you will love this. It is rich with butter and cream but unlike mousse, does not involve egg whites, so is heavier with a velvety texture. The great thing about it from an entertaining point of view is that there is no baking, as it sets into a loaf tin and can be left to chill in the refrigerator until you are ready to serve.

3 egg yolks

115 g caster sugar

200 g dark chocolate (minimum 70% cocoa solids), roughly broken into pieces

75 g unsalted butter, at room temperature

2 tablespoons cocoa powder

125 ml single cream

125 ml crème fraîche

2 small sweet oranges

1 small punnet blackberries, to serve

a loaf tin, 8 x 22 cm, lined with clingfilm

Serves 6–8

Put the egg yolks and sugar in a heatproof bowl and use a hand-held electric mixer to beat for 5 minutes, until pale and thick. Set the bowl over a saucepan of barely simmering water, making sure the bottom of the bowl does not come into contact with the water. Add the chocolate and stir as it melts. Add 1 tablespoon of the butter at a time and beat until well combined. Remove the bowl from the heat and gently fold in the cocoa powder. Leave to cool for about 10 minutes.

Put the cream and crème fraîche in a separate bowl and gently beat until soft peaks form. Fold about 65 ml of the cream mixture into the chocolate mixture, then add the remaining cream mixture. Spoon into the prepared loaf tin, cover and refrigerate overnight.

Peel the oranges, removing all the white pith, and slice them thinly. Pick over the blackberries and wash if necessary.

Remove the marquise from the refrigerator and carefully turn out onto a chilled serving platter. Cut into thick slices and serve with the orange slices and blackberries arranged on the side.

Chocolate truffles

These elegant cocoa-dusted truffles are a cinch to make and perfect for those guests who are in denial about wanting a 'real' dessert. Serve them with coffee, balancing one on the saucer of the cup, or arrange them on a plate and see how long they last.

200 g dark chocolate (minimum 70% cocoa solids)

5 tablespoons single cream

125 g unsalted butter, softened

2 teaspoons Grand Marnier or other flavoured liqueur (optional)

3 tablespoons unsweetened cocoa powder, sifted

a melon baller

Makes about 36

Break the chocolate into pieces. Put it in a heatproof bowl with the cream and butter. Set the bowl over a saucepan of barely simmering water, making sure the base of the bowl does not come into contact with the water. Let the chocolate and butter melt, stirring often, until glossy.

Remove from the heat and stir in the Grand Marnier. Transfer to a clean, non-reactive dish and refrigerate for 3 hours until firm.

Chill 2 large plates. Sprinkle the cocoa powder onto one of the plates. Dip a melon baller into warm water and use it to scoop out a small ball of the chocolate mixture. Put it on the plate with the cocoa and roll the ball around until evenly coated in cocoa.

Transfer the ball to the second chilled plate and repeat to make about 36 truffles. Keep refrigerated until ready to serve. The truffles will keep for up to 1 week if stored in the fridge in an airtight container.

White chocolate pots

This is a simple yet indulgent treat that uses just three ingredients. It's very rich indeed, so just a small portion is all that's needed to satisfy even the most sweet-toothed of guests.

100 g good white chocolate

½ vanilla pod

200 ml double cream

fresh mixed summer berries, to serve (optional)

6 small cups, pots or ramekins

Serves 4–6

Break the chocolate into pieces and put it in a heatproof bowl.

Rub the vanilla pod between your palms to soften it then use a sharp knife to split it open lengthways. Scrape the seeds directly into the bowl with the chocolate.

Set the bowl over a saucepan of barely simmering water, making sure the bottom of the bowl does not come into contact with the water. Let the chocolate slowly melt then remove the bowl from the heat and stir the chocolate until smooth.

Put the cream in a bowl and whisk until thick and soft peaks form. Fold the cream into the melted chocolate.

Spoon the mixture into cups and refrigerate for at least 6 hours before serving. Serve on its own or with summer berries, if liked.

Cherry and walnut brownies

A rich, dense and gooey chocolate brownie is always a crowd pleaser and a great way to end a meal. The fruit and nut combination in these brownies gives them a rather festive feel, especially if served with cream.

350 g caster sugar

80 g cocoa powder

60 g plain flour

1 teaspoon baking powder

200 g dark chocolate (minimum 70% cocoa solids)

4 eggs, beaten

100 g fresh cherries, stoned and halved

200 g walnut halves

250 g unsalted butter, melted

single cream or vanilla ice cream, to serve

a 20-cm square brownie tin or similar, greased and lined with baking parchment

Serves 10–12

Preheat the oven to 170°C (325°F) Gas 3.

Put the sugar in a large bowl. Sift in the cocoa powder, flour and baking powder. Chop the chocolate.

Add the eggs and mix until just combined. Stir in the chocolate pieces, cherries and walnuts. Put the butter in a small saucepan and set over very low heat to melt. Pour the melted butter into the mixture and stir in, but without overmixing.

Spoon the mixture into the prepared tin and bake in the preheated oven for 45 minutes. Leave to cool for at least 30 minutes before cutting into squares. Serve with chilled cream or vanilla ice cream, as preferred.

Blueberry madeleines with little lemon creams

A favourite in the pâtisseries of France, delicate madeleine cakes are traditionally baked in a tin with shell-shaped holes. The little lemon creams are really 'possets'; a traditional English dessert that uses the natural citric acid present in lemons to set the cream. It is smooth and velvety, almost butter-like, and offers a nice contrast in texture to the golden sponge cakes with their tart blueberries.

2 eggs

65 g unrefined caster sugar

100 g plain flour

75 g unsalted butter, melted and cooled

50 g fresh blueberries, frozen until firm

icing sugar, for dusting

Lemon cream

125 ml single cream

125 ml double cream

65 g caster sugar

2 tablespoons freshly squeezed lemon juice

6 small wine or liqueur glasses

a 12-hole madeleine tin, greased and lightly dusted with flour

Serves 6

To make the lemon cream, put both the creams in a saucepan and add the caster sugar. Set over medium heat and cook, stirring often, until the mixture starts to boil around the edge. Reduce the heat to medium/low and let the cream gently bubble for about 3 minutes. Remove from the heat and stir in the lemon juice. Let sit for 10 minutes. Stir just once and pour the mixture into the serving glasses. Refrigerate for at least 6 hours, until set.

Preheat the oven to 200°C (400°F) Gas 6.

Put the eggs and caster sugar in a bowl and use a hand-held mixer to beat for about 5 minutes, until pale and thick.

Sift in the flour and add the butter and blueberries. Spoon the mixture into the prepared tin and bake in the preheated oven for 12–15 minutes, until the cakes are golden and spring back when gently pressed in the centre. Leave the cakes to cool in the tin and dust liberally with icing sugar. Serve 2 cakes per person with a glass of lemon cream and a teaspoon.

Baked cheesecake

160 g very dry, slightly sweet biscuits, such as Rich Tea or Arnott's Coffee Biscuits

225 g caster sugar

100 g unsalted butter

750 g full-fat cream cheese

5 eggs

300 ml soured cream

1 teaspoon finely grated lemon zest

a 23-cm springform cake tin, lined with baking parchment and lightly greased with butter

kitchen foil

Serves 8–10

Preheat the oven to 170°C (325°F) Gas 3. Wrap the entire outside of the prepared cake tin in 2 layers of kitchen foil.

Put the biscuits and 1 tablespoon of the sugar in a food processor and process to a fine crumb. Add the melted butter and process until well combined. Tip the crumb mixture into the prepared tin and spread evenly over the base. Use the bottom of a glass tumbler to firmly press the crumb mixture into the tin. Bake in the preheated oven for 20 minutes. Remove and leave to cool completely.

Put the cream cheese and remaining sugar in a bowl, preferably that of a free-standing electric mixer with a paddle attachment, and beat for 2 minutes, until smooth and well combined. Add the eggs, one at a time, beating well between each addition and scraping down the side of the mixer bowl. Add the lemon zest and soured cream. Beat until the mixture is smooth.

Pour the mixture into the prepared tin and level the top with a palette knife. Bake in the still-hot oven for 1 hour, until the top of the cheesecake is golden but the centre is still wobbly. Turn the oven off and partially open the oven door. Leave the cheesecake to cool in the oven for 1 hour. Refrigerate for 6 hours, or ideally overnight.

Remove the cheesecake from the refrigerator 1 hour before eating. When ready to serve, run a warm, dry knife around the edge of the cake and remove the springform side. Cut into generous wedges to serve.

Who doesn't love a good baked cheesecake? Make this the day before you want to serve it and don't worry about cracks in the surface – it will still taste wonderful! For the best results, bring the cream cheese, eggs and soured cream to room temperature before using.

Spiced muscat figs

250 ml muscat (or other sweet dessert wine)

125 g caster sugar

1 vanilla pod

2 cardamom pods, lightly crushed

2 strips of orange zest from an unwaxed orange

8 fresh green figs

vanilla ice cream, to serve (optional)

Serves 4

Muscat is a grape variety that produces deliciously sweet and syrupy dessert wines known as moscato in Italy and moscatel in Spain. Whichever one you choose, the result will be the same – a deliciously fragrant and light dessert that will wow your guests.

Put the muscat, sugar, vanilla and cardamom pods and orange zest in a medium saucepan and set over high heat. Bring the mixture to the boil, then reduce the heat to medium. Add the figs to the pan, cover and cook for 20–25 minutes, until the figs are very tender. Remove the figs from the pan with a slotted spoon and set aside.

Return the liquid to the boil and cook for about 8–10 minutes, until thick and syrupy.

Serve 2 figs per person, with the syrup spooned over the top. Serve with a scoop of vanilla ice cream, if liked.

Flan casero

450 g sugar

1 litre whole milk

2 teaspoons vanilla extract

10 eggs

an ovenproof frying pan

a roasting tin, large enough to fit the frying pan in

Serves 10–12

This is basically a giant crème caramel, and as such is Spain's most popular dessert, where it is on every menu in every region. And rightly so, as the simple, yet delicious combination of rich baked egg custard with a caramelized sugar syrup is a real winner and everyone will want second helpings.

Put half of the sugar in a large, heavy-based frying pan and set over medium heat. Cook until the sugar has dissolved and is just starting to turn golden around the sides of the pan. Increase the heat to high and gently swirl the pan over the heat so the sugar dissolves and is the colour of golden syrup or honey. Remove the pan from the heat before the sugar starts to burn and continue swirling the pan so that the side is covered in the caramel. Do this until the caramel starts to set. Set aside until needed.

Preheat the oven to 180°C (350°F) Gas 4. Carefully put the frying pan with the caramel into a large roasting tin.

Put the milk and vanilla extract in a large saucepan and heat over medium heat until the milk reaches boiling point, but remove it from the heat just before it boils.

Put the eggs and remaining sugar in a bowl and whisk until well combined. Add the hot milk to the egg mixture and whisk to combine. Strain the mixture through a fine sieve, then pour the custard into the frying pan, over the caramel. Pour enough cold water into the roasting tin to come almost to the top of the frying pan and carefully put into the preheated oven.

Cook for 1¼ hours, until the custard has set. It may still be slightly wobbly in the centre. Lift the frying pan out of the roasting tin and let it sit at room temperature until cool. Refrigerate for 3 hours or ideally overnight.

To serve, run a knife around the side of the frying pan, to remove any stuck-on bits. Sit a serving plate, larger than the frying pan, over the top and quickly turn the flan out onto the plate. Sit it on a work surface and tap the bottom of the frying pan to release the flan. Use a large spoon to serve.

Zabaglione with summer fruits

Zabaglione is a classic Italian dessert that combines a few simple ingredients to stunning effect. It needs to be made at the very last minute, so it will keep you in the kitchen for a short while, but it is well worth the effort. Strawberries, peaches and nectarines are used here, as they taste and look so good together, but any combination of your favourite summer fruits will work. Serve with small glasses of a floral dessert wine alongside this.

220 g granulated sugar

2 nectarines, stoned and cut into thick wedges

2 peaches, stoned and cut into thick wedges

500 g fresh strawberries, hulled

Zabaglione

4 egg yolks

60 g caster sugar

100 ml Marsala or sweet sherry

Serves 4–6

Put the granulated sugar in a large saucepan with 750 ml water and set over high heat. Bring to the boil and boil for 5 minutes. Remove from the heat and let cool completely.

Put the fruit in a non-reactive bowl and pour the cooled syrup over the top. Cover and chill for 3–6 hours.

To make the zabaglione, put the egg yolks, caster sugar and Marsala in a large heatproof bowl. Set the bowl over a saucepan of barely simmering water, making sure the bottom of the bowl does not come into contact with the water.

Use a balloon whisk or hand-held electric whisk to beat gently for a few minutes, until well combined, then beat more vigorously for about 8–10 minutes, until the mixture has doubled in volume and is thick and spoonable.

Use a slotted spoon to transfer the fruit to a serving platter and spoon the warm zabaglione over the top. Serve immediately.

Strawberry tiramisù

400 g fresh strawberries

5 amaretti biscuits

2 large eggs, separated

40 g unrefined caster sugar

¼ teaspoon vanilla extract

4 tablespoons white rum

250 g mascarpone cheese, at room temperature

3 tablespoons whipping cream

100 ml pressed apple juice

½ a 200-g pack savoiardi (sponge finger biscuits)

a large, deep-sided glass bowl

Serves 6

This is an adaptation of the popular dessert, given a light summery twist with the addition of fresh strawberries, crunchy amaretti biscuits and rum.

Hull the strawberries. Weigh out 100 g and chop them finely. Slice the remaining strawberries and set aside.

Put the amaretti biscuits in a polythene bag, seal, then bash them with a rolling pin until they look like coarse breadcrumbs.

Beat the egg yolks in a bowl with an electric hand-held mixer or a whisk until pale yellow and fluffy, gradually adding the sugar as you go. Add the vanilla extract and a tablespoon of the rum. Tip the mascarpone cheese into a large bowl, beat with a wooden spoon to soften, then gradually add the egg yolk mixture and beat until smooth. In another bowl, whisk the egg whites until they just hold a soft peak. Fold the chopped strawberries into the mascarpone cheese mixture, then carefully fold in the egg whites.

Whip the whipping cream then fold that in too, together with a third of the crushed amaretti biscuits. Mix the remaining rum with the apple juice. Dip some of the savoiardi in the apple-rum mixture and lay across the base of your bowl. Reserving some sliced strawberries for decoration, arrange a layer of strawberries over the biscuits, then cover with a layer of mascarpone cream. Repeat with 1 or 2 more layers of soaked biscuits, strawberries and mascarpone cream, finishing with the mascarpone cream. Cover the bowl with clingfilm and chill in the fridge for 5 hours.

About 1 hour before serving, sprinkle the remaining amaretti biscuits over the top of the tiramisù and decorate with the remaining strawberries. Return it to the fridge until you are ready to serve.

Chocolate orange mousse

This is an adults-only version of a classic chocolate mousse – it's very rich and slightly tipsy. Chocolate and orange are a match made in heaven, so make sure you don't omit the Grand Marnier, which will complement the dark chocolate beautifully.

1 teaspoon finely grated orange zest from an unwaxed orange

2 tablespoons Grand Marnier or other orange-flavoured liqueur

250 g good-quality dark chocolate (at least 70% cocoa solids), roughly chopped

4 eggs, separated

250 ml single cream, whipped to soft peaks

chopped pistachios, to serve

6 individual serving dishes or wine glasses

Serves 6

Put the orange zest, Grand Marnier and chocolate in a heatproof bowl set over a saucepan of barely simmering water. Do not let the base of the bowl touch the water. Stir occasionally, until the chocolate has melted and the mixture is smooth and glossy.

Remove the bowl from the heat, leave the mixture to cool for 5 minutes, then beat in the egg yolks one at a time. Put the egg whites in a separate, grease-free bowl and whisk until softly peaking, taking care not to overbeat them. Gently fold the whisked egg whites into the chocolate mixture in two batches, then fold in the whipped cream until well combined.

Spoon the mixture into 6 individual serving dishes. Cover each one with clingfilm and chill in the fridge for at least 3 hours. Sprinkle over the chopped pistachios just before serving.

Rhubarb and custard pots

These are very pretty desserts, perfect for entertaining, as they can be made well in advance and popped in the fridge until you are ready to serve. Early forced rhubarb is more tender and will cook much more quickly than the later, ruby-coloured stalks. It's a good idea to keep your eye on it as it cooks as you don't want a pink mush, but rather a softly poached fruit that's still intact. The method here will give you a custard that is silky smooth, but if you prefer a thicker custard, simply cook it for a bit longer, until it coats the back of a wooden spoon.

600 g rhubarb, chopped into 3-cm lengths

3 tablespoons caster sugar

1 teaspoon finely grated orange zest from
an unwaxed orange

2 tablespoons freshly squeezed orange juice

Vanilla custard

250 ml single cream

250 ml double cream

1 vanilla pod, split in half lengthways

4 egg yolks

2 tablespoons caster sugar

2 tablespoons toasted flaked almonds

6 *individual serving dishes*

Serves 6

Put the rhubarb, sugar, orange zest and juice in a saucepan with
2 tablespoons cold water and set over high heat. Cook, stirring
constantly, until the mixture boils. Reduce the heat to medium
and simmer for 5 minutes, until the rhubarb is soft but still retains
some shape. Spoon the rhubarb into the serving dishes and set
aside to cool while you make the custard.

Put both the single and double creams in a saucepan. Set over
low heat and add the vanilla pod. Slowly bring the cream to the
boil. As the cream boils, remove the pod and scrape the seeds
into the custard using the tip of a sharp knife. Discard the bean.

Put the egg yolks and sugar in a bowl and whisk for 1 minute.
Slowly pour the hot cream into the yolk mixture, whisking
constantly. Transfer the mixture to a clean saucepan and set over
low heat. Cook for 5 minutes, being careful not to let it boil.

While still warm, spoon the custard over the rhubarb and let
the pots chill in the fridge for at least 3 hours or overnight.

Grape and lemon mascarpone tart

This is a really simple dessert that you can make with a ready-rolled pastry base. A gorgeous tangy Italian lemon liqueur gives a sharp edge to the creamy mascarpone.

230 g ready-rolled puff pastry, thawed if frozen

2 large eggs, separated

2 tablespoons unrefined caster sugar, plus 1 teaspoon for sprinkling

250 g mascarpone

2½ tablespoons limoncello (Italian lemon liqueur)

250 g white seedless grapes, rinsed and dried

250 g red seedless grapes, rinsed and dried

1 teaspoon icing sugar

a large baking tray, lightly greased

Serves 6–8

Preheat the oven to 200°C (400°F) Gas 6.

Take the pastry out of the fridge and leave it to rest for 20 minutes. Unroll and lift carefully onto the prepared baking tray. Using a dinner plate as a template, trim around the edge with a sharp knife to make a round of about 28 cm diameter.

Lightly whisk the egg whites and brush a thin layer onto the pastry. Sprinkle with 1 teaspoon sugar, then use the tines of a fork to prick the pastry all over. Bake in the preheated oven for 10–12 minutes, until puffed up and brown. Leave to cool while you make the topping.

Tip the mascarpone into a bowl and gradually work in the limoncello. Using a hand-held electric mixer, beat the egg yolks with the remaining caster sugar until pale, thick and creamy. Gently fold the mascarpone mixture into the eggs until thoroughly blended.

Transfer the cooled pastry base to a large serving plate. Spread over the mascarpone mixture with a spatula, taking it almost to the edges. Scatter the grapes on top, sift over the icing sugar and serve immediately.

Apricot tart with Muscat de Beaumes-de-Venise

This is a brilliantly simple recipe – if you've never made a tart in your life, you could make this. It looks fabulous and is guaranteed to impress your guests.

375-g pack ready-rolled puff pastry, thawed if frozen

750 g ripe apricots

2 tablespoons ground almonds

2 tablespoons unrefined caster sugar

2 tablespoons Muscat de Beaumes-de-Venise

3 tablespoons soft-set apricot jam

Greek yoghurt or vanilla ice cream, to serve

a shallow, rectangular, non-stick baking tin

Serves 6

Preheat the oven to 225°C (425°F) Gas 7. Take the pastry out of the fridge about 10 minutes before you want to unroll it.

Halve and stone the apricots. Unroll the pastry and lay it on the baking tin, trimming off any pastry that overhangs the edges. Prick the base with the tines of a fork and sprinkle over the ground almonds in an even layer, followed by about 1 tablespoon of the sugar. Arrange the apricot halves in rows over the surface of the pastry, leaving a narrow border around the edge and propping up each row on the one behind it. Spoon over the remaining sugar. Bake in the preheated oven for 30–35 minutes until the pastry is risen and the edges of the fruit are beginning to caramelize.

Spoon the jam into a small saucepan, add the Muscat and warm gently over low heat, stirring until smooth. Brush the warm glaze over the apricots. Serve the tart in slices with double cream or vanilla ice cream.

Fresh raspberry and almond slices

150 g fresh raspberries, frozen until firm

1 egg

3 tablespoons caster sugar

1 tablespoon plain flour

75 g unsalted butter

chilled cream, to serve (optional)

Almond shortcrust pastry

50 g ground almonds

200 g plain flour

80 g caster sugar

125 g unsalted butter, chilled and cubed

a rectangular tart tin (about 37 x 10 cm), lightly greased

Serves 6–8

These taste better the day after they are baked, which makes them ideal for making ahead of time. If you want to eat them warm, reheat in a low oven before serving.

Preheat the oven to 180°C (350°F) Gas 4.

To make the pastry, put the ground almonds, flour and sugar in a food processor. With the motor running, add a cube of butter at a time until it is all incorporated and the mixture resembles coarse breadcrumbs. Add 2 tablespoons cold water and process until just combined. Be careful not to overprocess.

Tip the pastry out onto a lightly-floured work surface and knead to form a ball. Roll it out between 2 layers of baking parchment until it is about 5 cm longer and 5 cm wider than the tart tin. Carefully lift the pastry into the tin and use your fingers to press it down into the base and sides, letting it overhang. Prick the base all over with the tines of a fork and bake in the preheated oven for 20 minutes, until lightly golden. Break off the overhanging pastry.

Put the egg, sugar and flour in a bowl and use a balloon whisk to beat until thick and pale. Put the butter in a small saucepan and set over medium heat. Leave to melt until frothy and dark golden with a nutty aroma. Working quickly, pour the melted butter over the egg mixture and beat well. Scatter the raspberries in the tart case. Pour the warm batter over the raspberries. Bake in the still-hot oven for about 45 minutes, until the top resembles a golden meringue. Leave to cool for 30 minutes before serving. Cut into slices and serve with chilled cream, if liked.

Pear, almond and mascarpone tart

This indulgent recipe works best if the pears are on the overripe side so that they are fork-tender when cooked. If time is short you can use ready-made shortcrust pastry.

4 very ripe pears

1 tablespoon freshly squeezed lemon juice

4 tablespoons caster sugar

125 g mascarpone

1 egg

1 tablespoon plain flour

100 g flaked almonds

2 tablespoons unrefined sugar

chilled cream, to serve

Pastry

200 g plain flour

4 tablespoons caster sugar

80 g unsalted butter, chilled and cubed

a 24-cm loose-bottomed tart tin, lightly greased and floured

Serves 8–10

To make the pastry, put the flour and caster sugar in a food processor and pulse to combine. With the motor running, add the butter and 1–2 tablespoons cold water and mix until the mixture resembles coarse breadcrumbs and starts to gather in lumps. Transfer to a lightly-floured work surface and briefly knead to form a ball. Wrap in clingfilm and chill in the fridge for 1 hour, until firm.

Preheat the oven to 180°C (350°F) Gas 4.

Coarsely grate the chilled pastry into a large bowl. Using lightly floured hands, scatter the grated pastry into the prepared tart tin and use your fingers to gently press it in, until the entire base and the side of the tin are covered. Bake in the preheated oven for about 25 minutes, until lightly golden. Leave to cool.

Peel, halve and core the pears. Put them in a non-reactive bowl with the lemon juice and 1 tablespoon of the caster sugar. Put the remaining caster sugar in a food processor. Add the mascarpone, egg and flour and process to form a thick paste.

Spread the mixture over the pastry. Arrange the pears on top and scatter with the almonds and raw sugar. Bake in the still-hot oven for 40–45 minutes, until the pears are soft and the mascarpone mixture has set. Serve warm with chilled cream for pouring.

Messy strawberries Romanoff

This is a foolproof dessert that pays homage to a popular fine dining dessert from the 1970s. Meringues are roughly broken and arranged on a serving platter, then topped with lightly whipped cream and Cointreau-macerated ripe strawberries.

500 g fresh strawberries, hulled

65 ml Cointreau or other orange-flavoured liqueur

6 bought meringue nests

125 ml single or whipping cream

4 tablespoons icing sugar, plus extra for dusting

Serves 4

Put the strawberries in a non-reactive bowl and add the Cointreau. Cover and leave to sit at room temperature for 3 hours, stirring often.

Roughly break each meringue into 3–4 pieces and arrange them on a serving platter.

Put the cream in a grease-free bowl and use a hand held electric mixer to whip. Add the icing sugar, a little at a time, as you whip, until the mixture is softly peaking.

Spoon the cream over the meringue pieces then arrange the strawberries on top, along with 1–2 tablespoons of the macerating juice. Dust with icing sugar just before serving.

Variation: Try replacing the strawberries with raspberries or blackberries, or even sliced poached peaches, scattered with toasted flaked almonds.

Passion fruit pavlovas

A simple-to-assemble, fresh-tasting and impressive dessert, ideal for any special occasion.

4 fresh passion fruit

2 tablespoons freshly squeezed orange juice

2 teaspoons unrefined caster sugar, plus extra to taste

a few drops of orange flower water (optional)

4 bought meringue nests

4 heaped tablespoons lemon or orange curd (optional)

4 small scoops vanilla ice cream

Serves 4

Halve the passion fruit and scoop the pulp and seeds into a bowl, taking care not to remove any of the bitter pith.

Add the orange juice and sugar and stir. Check for sweetness, adding the orange flower water and/or extra sugar to taste.

Put a meringue nest on each plate and spoon the curd, if using, into the base. Top with a scoop of ice cream and spoon over the orange and passion fruit sauce. Serve immediately.

Roasted hazelnut and chocolate cake

1½ tablespoons cocoa powder

100 g shelled hazelnuts

125 g dark chocolate (minimum 70% cocoa solids), broken into pieces

1 tablespoon strong black espresso coffee

1 tablespoon brandy

100 g caster sugar

100 g unsalted butter

3 eggs, separated

cream, to serve (optional)

a 23-cm springform cake tin, greased and lined

Serves 8–10

There are very few ingredients in this fantastic recipe, so do use really good-quality chocolate, not only for flavour but also because the content of cocoa fat solids will influence the result. It has a very soft texture, so it's important to let it cool before slicing.

Preheat the oven to 170°C (325°F) Gas 3.

Sprinkle the cocoa powder into the prepared cake tin and gently tap the side and bottom of the tin until evenly coated.

Spread the hazelnuts out on a baking tray and roast in the preheated oven for 10 minutes, shaking the tray after 5 minutes, until the skins are dark. Remove from the oven and leave to cool completely. Wrap the hazelnuts in a clean tea towel and use the towel to rub the nuts vigorously, to remove as much skin as possible. Pick any remaining skin off the nuts and put them in a food processor. Process until very finely chopped. Set aside.

Put the chocolate, coffee and brandy in a heatproof bowl. Set the bowl over a saucepan of barely simmering water, making sure the base of the bowl does not touch the water. Let the chocolate melt, then remove from the heat and stir until smooth. Add the sugar, butter and egg yolks to the chocolate mixture in the warm bowl and beat until smooth. Transfer the mixture into a mixing bowl and fold in the roasted hazelnuts.

Put the egg whites in a grease-free bowl and use a hand-held electric mixer to whisk until stiffly peaking. Fold the egg whites into the chocolate mixture in two batches. Spoon the mixture into the prepared cake tin and bake in the still-hot oven for 20 minutes, until slightly risen yet still a little wobbly in the centre. Leave to cool to room temperature before serving in slices with chilled cream for pouring, if liked.

Chocolates, coffee and cognac

For a special occasion, you can serve this at the end of the meal, otherwise it makes a great substitute for a dessert. Source the best hand-made chocolates you can find, preferably made from dark chocolate, including some truffles for contrast. Brew up some real coffee – espresso for those who want it and an Americano for those who prefer a less intense brew – and serve with the best cognac or Spanish brandy you can afford.

Seasonal cheeseboards

It's time to change the way you think about cheeseboards, designing them, like other foods we serve, to reflect the seasons and our mood. It's an approach that makes perfect sense, as so many cheeses themselves are seasonal. Why serve the same board in June as you would in December?

It also helps to limit the number of cheeses you serve and pick them carefully. If you include a strong-smelling French cheese and a pungent blue in your selection, for example, you'll struggle to find a wine to go with them both. The traditional approach is to serve the widest range of cheeses you can afford, displaying your generosity as a host, but the chances are that your guests will enjoy the experience just as much if you select two or three that work together.

With the seasonal approach you can also be a bit more imaginative about the way you dress your cheeseboard, introducing accompaniments that will complement the flavour of your cheeses and reflect the time of year. Warm, rich dried fruits, for example, in winter when fresh fruits are less widely available; fresh salads in spring.

Finally, don't get too stuck on the idea that the only accompaniment for a cheeseboard is a glass of red wine. There are many other drinks that work just as well. Crisp white wines in spring, for example, or a glass of sweet sherry or Madeira rather than port. It's sometimes a great deal easier to find a Belgian beer to match a powerful cheese, and artisanal cider can also be a great pairing.

Spring

Spring and early summer is the ideal time of year to enjoy fresh young goats' cheeses and their perfect partner Sauvignon Blanc. Choose two or three cheeses for contrast: one young, light and moussey, one that has been matured a little longer and one that has been rolled in herbs. Serve them with a lightly dressed herb salad bought from the farmers' market. You could also add a wedge of tangy, fresh Italian pecorino and a few shelled broad beans, a delicious combination. Breads should be light too – slices of ciabatta and some crisp Italian flatbread such as 'carta di musica'. A good choice of Sauvignon would be a minerally Sancerre or Pouilly Fumé, but choose any unoaked Sauvignon that you enjoy.

Summer

Now the flavours are richer and fuller, begging for a full-bodied red wine. The type of cheese that works best are the smooth, tangy hard sheep's cheeses you traditionally find in Spain and the Basque region of France, full flavoured but without any touch of bitterness. I also like to add a Fleur de Maquis, a Corsican cheese rolled in rosemary and fennel. Add some other Mediterranean ingredients – a few chewy sun-dried tomatoes, some olives and olive bread – and you've got the perfect foil for a rich southern French red from the Languedoc or the Rhône, or a Spanish red such as a Rioja.

Autumn

The ploughman's lunch re-invented. Forget wine for once and turn to cider, the natural accompaniment for autumn fruits and flavours. Mix and match among ancient and modern British and Irish cheeses – a fine Cheddar, an Irish Adrahan or other washed-rind cheese, a snowy white-rinded Tunworth, maybe even a mellow blue. Serve with fine, flavourful eating apples and pears, a mild apple chutney (home-made or bought) and an old-fashioned white crusty loaf, and pour chunky glasses of cool, artisanal cider, offering your guests a choice of dry or medium-dry if you wish. You could even offer brandy glasses of Somerset Cider Brandy or Calvados to round off the meal.

Winter

Port and blue cheese are a classic pairing, but give it a modern twist. Serve three contrasting cheeses, say a Stilton, a Roquefort and a mild Gorgonzola or Harbourne Blue (a mild blue goats' cheese from Devon) and serve them with a top-class collection of dried fruits such as Medjool dates, figs or raisins and a handful of walnuts and brazil nuts. Echo the dried fruit flavours with a simple raisin and rosemary bread or a walnut bread, and introduce a little crunch with a few handcut oat biscuits or oatcakes. This is the perfect occasion to bring out a vintage port (which you'll need to decant) or serve a fine Sauternes or a sweet Tokay from Hungary. What blue cheeses need is sweetness.

drinks

Sidecar

The Sidecar, like many of the classic cocktails created in the 1920s, is attributed to the inventive genius of Harry McElhone, who founded Harry's New York Bar in Paris. It is said to have been created in honour of an eccentric military man who would roll up outside the bar in the sidecar of his chauffeur-driven motorcycle. It makes a refreshing aperitif.

50 ml brandy
20 ml freshly squeezed lemon juice
20 ml Cointreau
sugar, for the glass

Serves 1

Shake all the ingredients together over ice and strain into a chilled martini glass with a sugared edge. Serve immediately.

Negroni

The Negroni packs a powerful punch but still makes an elegant aperitif. For a drier variation, add a little more dry gin, but if a fruitier cocktail is more to your taste, wipe some orange zest around the top of the glass and drop into the drink.

25 ml Campari
25 ml sweet vermouth
25 ml dry gin
a strip of orange zest, to garnish

Serves 1

Build all the ingredients in a rocks glass filled with ice, garnish with the orange zest and stir. Serve immediately.

Perfect manhattan

'Perfect' does not refer to how well the drink is put together; it describes the perfect balance between sweet and dry.

50 ml rye whiskey

12.5 ml sweet vermouth

12.5 ml dry vermouth

2 dashes Angostura bitters

a strip of orange zest, to garnish

Serves 1

Add the ingredients to a mixing glass filled with ice (first ensure all the ingredients are very cold) and stir the mixture until chilled. Strain into a chilled cocktail glass, add the orange zest and serve immediately.

Original daiquiri

This classic cocktail was made famous at the El Floridita restaurant, Havana, early in the 20th century. Once you have found the perfect balance of golden rum, sharp citrus juice and sweet sugar syrup, stick to those measurements exactly.

50 ml golden rum (ideally Cuban)

20 ml freshly squeezed lime juice

2 barspoons sugar syrup (see page 141)
or gomme

Serves 1

Pour all the ingredients into a cocktail shaker filled with ice. Shake and strain into a chilled martini glass. Serve immediately.

Kir royale

After a shaky start, the Kir Royale is now the epitome of chic sophistication. It started life as the Kir, which contained acidic white wine instead of champagne, and was labelled rince cochon (French for 'pig rinse'). Luckily, the wine became less sharp and the drink adopted a more appropriate mantle.

1 dash crème de cassis

Champagne, to top up

Serves 1

Add a small dash of crème de cassis to a champagne flute and top up with Champagne. Stir gently and serve immediately.

Classic martini

This is a 'standard' martini. Stirring the cocktail rather than shaking it is the original labour of love for any bartender (and helps avoid chips of ice getting in this, the purest of drinks).

a dash of dry vermouth (Noilly Prat or
Martini Extra Dry)

75 ml well-chilled gin or vodka

a small green olive or lemon twist, to garnish

Serves 1

Add both the ingredients to a mixing glass filled with ice and stir. Strain into a chilled martini glass and garnish with an olive or lemon twist. Serve immediately.

Cosmopolitan

The Sex and the City franchise made this fun drink popular and its great taste has ensured that it stays that way!

35 ml lemon-flavoured vodka

20 ml triple sec

20 ml freshly squeezed lime juice

25 ml unsweetened cranberry juice

Serves 1

Add all the ingredients to a cocktail shaker filled with ice, shake sharply and strain into a chilled martini glass. Serve immediately.

Margarita

Pre-mixes, poor-quality tequila, too much ice and cordial instead of fresh lemon or lime juice all contribute to an unacceptable margarita. Follow this classic recipe and don't let your margaritas be tarred by the same brush!

50 ml gold tequila

25 ml triple sec or Cointreau

25 ml freshly squeezed lime juice

salt, for the glass

Serves 1

Put all the ingredients in a cocktail shaker and shake sharply with cracked ice, then strain into a chilled margarita glass edged with salt. Serve immediately.

Mojito

The Mojito has had a big revival. Even the great British pub has had a stab at making them. If you want to create the perfect Mojito, here's a great recipe.

2 lime wedges

2 teaspoons raw cane sugar

8 fresh mint sprigs, plus 1 to garnish

50 ml light rum

1 dash soda water

sugar syrup (see page 141), to taste

Serves 1

Crush (muddle) the lime, sugar and mint in the bottom of a highball glass, fill with plenty of crushed ice and add the rum. Stir well and add a dash of soda water. Add a dash or two of sugar syrup, to taste. Garnish with a mint sprig and serve immediately.

Blood orange and campari mimosa

Mimosa or Buck's Fizz is a standard offering at brunch gatherings, but this one is different. The Campari and blood orange make it a little bitter, and this really whets the appetite. Add a dash of sugar syrup or honey if you prefer a sweeter drink.

500 ml pure blood orange juice

2 tablespoons Campari

750-ml bottle sparkling white wine, chilled

Serves 4

Divide the blood orange juice between 4 champagne flutes. Add a dash of Campari to each one, then top up with the wine. Serve immediately.

Sea breeze

This is a great drink for summer. Simple to make, really refreshing and easy to make up in volume for a party..

a handful of ice cubes

150 ml pure pink grapefruit juice

300 ml pure cranberry juice

100 ml vodka

1 lime, cut into wedges

Serves 2

Put the ice in a cocktail shaker along with the juices and vodka. Squeeze over a couple of lime wedges. Put the top on the shaker and shake a few times. Strain into 2 tall glasses and add a lime wedge to each before serving.

Bloody mary

There's nothing like a good Bloody Mary after a late night: it seems to get the blood pumping and cure any feelings of drowsiness. If you want a Virgin Mary leave out the vodka but squeeze in some more lime for extra tanginess.

150 ml vodka

450 ml pure tomato juice

½ teaspoon hot horseradish sauce

1 teaspoon Worcestershire sauce

4 dashes Tabasco sauce

¼ teaspoon celery salt

½ teaspoon cracked black pepper

2 limes, cut into small wedges

ice cubes, to serve

Seerves 4

Mix all the ingredients together in a large jug. Taste and adjust the seasonings if necessary, adding more heat, pepper or lime as you wish. Add a couple of handfuls of ice and serve immediately.

wine with food

Food and wine matching made easy

If you've ever tasted a food you love with a wine that matches it perfectly, you'll know that the combination of the two can be even better than the food and wine on its own. But how to find those perfect pairings? The old 'white wine with fish, red wine with meat' rule is a bit dated, as anyone who has enjoyed a seared tuna steak with a Pinot Noir well knows. Wine has changed. Food has changed. The only rule is that there are no hard and fast rules, just combinations that most people are likely to enjoy.

Basically, there's no great mystique about it. Simply use your existing knowledge of food and think of wine as another ingredient you have to take into account when you're planning a meal – rather as you would when you choose a vegetable or sauce to serve on the side. The more food and wine matches you try, the more confident you'll feel, so take every opportunity to try out different combinations, particularly in restaurants that serve wines by the glass or suggest food and wine pairings with their menu. Here are some simple pointers that may help you:

• Match the wine to the sauce, not the basic ingredient. Chicken, for example, can be cooked in any number of different ways, so it's more useful to think about whether it's served in a creamy white wine and mushroom sauce (a smooth, dry white), a red wine sauce like coq au vin (a similar wine to the one you use to cook it), a Thai green curry sauce (a fruity, off-dry white) or a barbecue sauce or marinade (a ripe, fruity red).

• Think about the temperature and intensity of the dish. Dishes that are served raw or delicate, steamed dishes need lighter wines (usually white) than ones that are roasted, seared or grilled (more often red). Homemade dishes will often be more intensely seasoned than bought ones, so may need more intensely flavoured wines.

• Take into account what else is on the plate. Strongly flavoured vegetables, such as asparagus, red cabbage or beetroot, or fruity salsas and relishes, can make a difference to the wine you choose. If you served grilled salmon with asparagus, for instance, you'd probably go for a Sauvignon Blanc, while if you made a spicy mango salsa to go with it, go for a Semillion or Semillion-Chardonnay, or a fruity red.

• If you're serving several wines during a meal, you should generally start with lighter, drier wines and move on to richer, more full-bodied ones. Usually, that means white followed by red, but you could easily serve a full-bodied white with a main course or a lighter red followed by a more full-bodied one.

• Dessert wines need to be sweeter than the food they're accompanying, otherwise they can taste sharp.

• Stuck? Imagine wine as a fruit. If it's light and citrusy, it will go with dishes where you might think of adding a squeeze of lemon as you would to fried fish or chicken. If it has ripe red berry fruit flavours, it will probably go with ingredients to which you might think of adding red fruits such as duck, turkey or lamb. For more information on this topic, see Matching Wine to Food (page 180) and Matching Food to Wine (page 184).

Matching wine to food

Finding a precise match for a dish can be tricky because there are so many variables: how it is cooked, whether there are any strong spice or herbal accents, how many other ingredients there are on the plate. So, to make it as easy as possible, these lists concentrate on the style of food rather than individual dishes, but give specific examples where appropriate. They are intended as a guide and a starting point – don't be afraid to experiment!

SOUPS

You don't always need wine with a soup, as one liquid doesn't really need another. The thicker the soup, the easier it is to match.

Thin soups e.g. consommés or spicy South-East Asian broths are better without wine, although dry sherry will go with a traditional consommé.

Smooth creamy soups e.g. light vegetable soups: go for a smooth, dry, unoaked white such as Chablis or Soave.

Chunky soups should be treated as you would a stew – they can take a medium-bodied white or a red wine such as a Côtes du Rhône.

STARTERS

Given that they're served at the beginning of a meal, a crisp, dry white, aromatic white or rosé is generally most appropriate. Sometimes a light red can work too.

Cold, fish-based starters such as prawn or crab salads or terrines: a crisp, dry white such as Sancerre or other Loire Sauvignon Blanc, or a Riesling is good with smoked fish). Drink Chablis with oysters.

Hot, fish-based starters e.g. fishcakes or scallops: Chardonnay is usually a safe bet, except with spicy flavours when unoaked, fruity or aromatic whites work better.

Charcuterie (saucisson, salami, pâtés and air-dried hams): serve with dry rosé and light reds like Beaujolais.

Meat-based salads made with duck or chicken livers are best with Pinot Noir.

Cheese-based starters and cold quiches pair well with unoaked Chardonnay, while goats' cheese works well with Sauvignon Blanc. Champagne or sparkling wine pairs well with deep-fried camembert.

Vegetable-based starters e.g. terrines: follow similar recommendations to Cold Fish-based Starters. Asparagus works particularly well with Sauvignon Blanc.

Tapas chilled fino or manzanilla sherry.

PASTA, PIZZA AND NOODLES

It's not the type of pasta you use that determines your choice of wine, it's the sauce you put with it.

Creamy sauces e.g. spaghetti carbonara: smooth, dry, Italian unoaked whites such as Soave and Pinot Bianco.

Seafood-based sauces crisp, dry Italian whites and citrussy Sauvignon Blancs.

Tomato-based sauces fresh tomato sauces – crisp, dry whites such as Pinot Grigio or Sauvignon Blanc: cooked tomato sauces – a light Italian red such as Chianti or a Barbera.

Cheese-based sauces crisp, dry, intensely flavoured whites – good Pinot Grigio or a modern Sardinian white.

Rich meat or aubergine-based sauces e.g. Bolognese: a fruity Italian red such as a Barbera or a Sangiovese, or a southern Italian or Sicilian red.

Baked pasta dishes e.g. meat lasagne: a good Chianti.

Pizza generally, fruity Italian reds work better than whites, except with seafood pizzas.

Noodles generally spicy, so crisp fruity whites or aromatic whites such as Riesling tend to work best.

RICE DISHES

Rice dishes work in a similar way to pasta with wine.

Risotto Most light vegetable- and seafood-based risottos pair well with crisp, dry whites such as good-quality Pinot Grigio or Soave and with sparkling wines like Champagne. Richer risottos based on dried mushrooms (porcini) or beetroot can take a red (Pinot Noir and Dolcetto respectively).

Spicy rice (e.g. paella, jambalaya): dry southern French or Spanish rosé and tempranillo-based reds such as those from Rioja and Navarra.

Sushi Muscadet or dry Champagne, especially Blanc de Blancs.

FISH

Cooked simply, fish is quite delicate, but more robust cooking techniques and saucing can call for more powerful wines.

Raw fish e.g. sushi, sashimi: see notes for Sushi, above.

Pickled fish e.g. herring: lager, especially a pilsener, works better with pickled fish than wine.

Oily fish e.g. mackerel, sardines: sharp, lemony whites such as Rueda and modern Greek whites.

Smoked fish: dry Riesling or Spanish manzanilla sherry.

Salmon served cold – unoaked Chardonnay e.g. Chablis; served hot in a pie or with pastry – lightly-oaked Chardonnay; with a hot butter sauce – a richer Chardonnay; seared or marinated with a spicy crust – a light red such as Pinot Noir.

Tuna served cold in salad – Sauvignon Blanc or dry rosé; seared or barbecued, go with a chilled Pinot Noir.

Fish in a creamy sauce including fish pie: lightly oaked Chardonnay, Chenin Blanc or oaked white Bordeaux.

Pan-fried or grilled fish If simply prepared this is an occasion to drink good white Burgundy or other top-quality Chardonnay or a clean-flavoured white like Albariño.

Fish and chips and other fried fish: crisp, dry whites such as Sauvignon Blanc or a sparkling wine.

Seared, roasted or barbecued fish can often take a light red, such as Pinot Noir, especially if wrapped in pancetta or served with lentils or beans.

BIRDS AND GAME

Chicken Being a neutrally flavoured bird, you need to focus more on the way chicken is cooked and the sauce that accompanies it than the chicken itself.

Roast chicken Good white or red Burgundy or quality New World Chardonnay or Pinot Noir; softer, riper styles of Bordeaux e.g. Pomerol and Merlot.

Grilled or chargrilled chicken This will depend on the baste or marinade; lighter, citrussy, herbal flavours suggest a crisp, fruity white like a Sauvignon Blanc; a spicier, sweeter marinade would work better with a jammy red like a Shiraz. With tomatoes, peppers and olives: a fruity, Italian red or other Sangiovese.

Coq au vin and other red wine sauces A similar red wine to the one you use to make the dish (a robust Rhône or Languedoc red or a Syrah).

Fried chicken Unoaked or lightly oaked Chardonnay.

Sweet and sour or fruity sauces Fruity Australian whites such as Semillon, Semillon-Chardonnay or Colombard, or ripe, fruity reds such as Merlot.

Chicken salads Depends a bit on the dressing. An unoaked Chardonnay or a fruity rosé will cover most eventualities but if there's a South-East Asian twist to the recipe, a Sauvignon Blanc, Riesling, Verdelho or Viognier is likely to work much better.

Turkey (see Chicken), but bear in mind that on festive occasions a roast turkey is likely to be accompanied by a flavoursome stuffing, fruity cranberry sauce and richly flavoured vegetables such as parsnips and butternut squash, which call for a more full-bodied red than a plain roast chicken: something like a fruity Pinot Noir, Shiraz or even Châteauneuf-du-Pape.

Duck Pinot Noir almost always works except with duck confit, which is better with a darker, more full-bodied southern French or Spanish red.

MEAT

Pork Very similar in flavour to chicken, but the extra fattiness calls for wines with a little more acidity. See also the sauces listed under Chicken, Pasta and Spicy Food.

Roast pork If flavoured Italian-style with garlic and fennel, choose a dry Italian white. Otherwise try a soft, fruity red such as a Pinot Noir, Merlot or a good Beaujolais. Chenin Blanc and Riesling are good with cold roast pork.

Pork with apples and cider Cider is a better choice than wine here.

Sausages Robust, fruity southern French or Spanish red.

Hot gammon A fruity red such as Merlot or a Carmenère.

Cold ham Chablis or other unoaked Chardonnay and Beaujolais. (See also notes for Charcuterie.)

Lamb Roast or grilled lamb: a good partner for a serious red, particularly red Bordeaux and other Cabernet- and Merlot-based wines, Rioja and Chianti Classico.

Lamb shanks and casseroles: Robust, rustic reds such as those from the Rhône, Southern France and Spain.

Greek-style lamb kebabs with mint and lemon can be partnered with a fruity red but equally good with a citrussy white.

Lamb tagines Rioja Reserva or soft, pruney southern Italian reds. See also notes for Spicy Foods.

Beef and venison Roasts and steaks: any fine red you enjoy. Argentinian Malbec is a particularly good steak wine.

Casseroles, stews and pies can cover quite a wide range of flavours from a beef stew with dumplings (for which beer is a better accompaniment than wine) to a rich oxtail stew (try Zinfandel). A useful guide is that if you use wine to make the stew, drink a robust red; if you use beer, drink ale.

Teriyaki or stir-fried beef A ripe fruity red such as a Chilean or Australian Cabernet Sauvignon or a full-bodied New World Pinot Noir. See also Spicy Foods.

Veal For many dishes recommendations would be similar to those for pork although given the cost of veal, you might feel justified in indulging in a rather better bottle of wine!

Veal escalopes Dry Italian whites such as Pinot Grigio or a red like Chianti.

Osso buco Italian dry whites, such as Soave, just have the edge on reds.

SPICY FOOD

Spice is not the enemy of wine that it's reputed to be, so long as you avoid wines that are very tannic. It's only really hot chillies that cause a problem.

Mildly spiced dishes including Middle-Eastern mezze, grills and mild Indian curries: simple, crisp fruity whites and dry rosés work best. See also Lamb Tagines.

Moderately hot curries such as Rogan Josh: Inexpensive fruity New World reds such as Cabernet-Shiraz blends. With chicken curries try a bottle of Semillon-Chardonnay.

Hot curries These are tricky but try Gewürztraminer or Pinotage. Otherwise stick to lager or the Indian drink lassi.

Smoked chilli, paprika or pimentón-based dishes such as chili con carne, goulash or bean dishes flavoured with chorizo: Soft, fruity reds such as Rioja, other aged Spanish reds and Zinfandel.

Thai salads and South-east Asian curries These are better with whites than reds. Alsace Riesling and Tokay Pinot Gris work well, as does Gewürztraminer especially with red Thai curries.

VEGETABLES

Vegetables are no different from any other ingredient – you need to think about the way they're cooked when you're debating what to drink. They are, however, more seasonal than other foods, so the time of year may affect your wine choice.

Spring vegetables and salads e.g. asparagus, peas and broad beans: crisp fresh, fruity whites such as Sauvignon Blanc and Grüner Veltliner.

Summer vegetables e.g. Mediterranean vegetables such as tomatoes, peppers, aubergines and courgettes: dry rosés and medium-bodied southern French and Italian reds.

Autumn vegetables e.g. sweetcorn, squash, pumpkin and mushrooms: a buttery Chardonnay goes particularly well with the first three. A lighter Chardonnay or Pinot Noir are both good choices with mushrooms.

Winter vegetables e.g. onions, carrots, parsnips and dark leafy greens: often served in hearty dishes such as stews and soups, which tend to suit rustic reds and ales.

Vegetarian dishes e.g. vegetarian bakes that contain beans or cheese again suit hearty reds, but you will need to check that they are suitable for vegetarians (i.e. that no animal-derived products have been used in making them).

CHEESE

Red wine isn't always the best choice with cheese, as explained on pages 163–165.

Goats' cheese Go for Sauvignon Blanc and English dry whites.

Camembert and brie-style cheeses Choose fruity reds such as Pinot Noir and Merlot. Cider is particularly good with Camembert.

Cheddar and other hard cheeses These are best with aged Spanish reds such as Rioja.

Strong washed-rind cheeses such as Epoisses and Munster – strong Belgian beers work better than wine, although Gewürztraminer is a classic pairing for Munster.

Blue cheeses Sweet wines, port or sweeter sherries.

Hot cheese dishes White wines generally work better than reds, unless it's a baked pasta dish like lasagne. With a fondue you need a really crisp, dry white like a Chasselas from Switzerland. With a macaroni cheese, try a light Chardonnay.

DESSERTS

You may not always want to serve a dessert wine, but there are some luscious pairings to experience.

Apple, pear, peach and apricot-based desserts Simple French-style fruit tarts are the perfect foil for a great dessert wine like Sauternes. Apricot tarts work well with sweet Muscat.

Strawberry and raspberry desserts These need light, lemony dessert wines with good acidity like late-harvest Sauvignon and Riesling. Strawberries can be macerated in a light, fruity red wine such as Beaujolais.

Lemon-flavoured desserts These can be tricky, especially if intensely lemony. Very sweet German and Austrian dessert wines tend to work best. Serving cream with them helps.

Light, creamy desserts e.g. gâteaux and pavlovas: serve with demi-sec Champagne or Moscato d'Asti.

Toffee- or caramel-flavoured desserts e.g. tarte tatin, pecan pie: late-harvested and liqueur Muscats work well with these.

Chocolate desserts: sweet reds are often easier to match than sweet whites

Matching food to wine

Sometimes the starting point for a meal is not a menu but a wine: a treasured bottle that you've been waiting for an occasion to drink or a gift that you want to share with the giver. Here are a few general points worth bearing in mind. Keep the food as simple and unfussy as possible and let the wine be the hero! If the wine is very old, you may find when you open it that it's past its best so always have a back-up. Younger wines of a very high quality may still be quite tannic and need some aeration, so you may find it pays to decant them. Build the meal around your special wine – if it's an outstanding red or a dessert wine, don't ply your guests with so much drink beforehand that they won't appreciate it.

WHITES

Chardonnay Lighter styles such as Chablis and good white Burgundy are perfect for simply prepared grilled fish, or delicate shellfish like scallops or prawns. Richer Chardonnays are fabulous with roast or sautéed chicken or veal, especially with wild mushrooms, creamy or buttery sauces or autumnal vegetables like butternut squash and pumpkin.

Sauvignon Blanc Unoaked Sauvignon is perfect for fresh-tasting fish dishes such as grilled seabass, spring vegetables (especially asparagus), and goats' cheese. Oaked Sauvignons, especially those that are blended with Semillon as in Bordeaux, work with similar dishes to Chardonnay.

Riesling Dry rieslings are shown off best by delicate seafood like fresh crab, prawns and lightly smoked fish such as trout or salmon. Sweeter styles are good with duck, goose and subtly spiced Asian dishes.

Pinot Grigio/Pinot Gris Pinot Grigio is a good choice for antipasti, seafood-based pasta or risotto, and simply grilled fish. Richer Pinot Gris, which often has a note of sweetness, works better with lightly spiced chicken and pork dishes, especially if they have a South-East Asian twist.

Viognier Works with similar dishes to Chardonnay but can handle more spice.

Gewürztraminer This exotically scented white isn't to everyone's taste, but it comes into its own with spicy food, especially Thai and moderately spiced Indian curries. It's also good with duck.

REDS

Pinot Noir e.g. red Burgundy Duck is a great choice with young fruity Pinot Noir as is roasted chicken and turkey and seared tuna. Older Pinots are good with guinea fowl and game birds such as pheasant.

Cabernet Sauvignon, Merlot and blends of the two e.g. red Bordeaux You can't go wrong with roast beef or lamb, a steak or some grilled lamb chops. If you're dealing with an older vintage, keep any sauces and side dishes light

Syrah/shiraz French Syrahs such as those from the Northern Rhône are good with red meat, but can take more robust treatment – intensely flavoured winey stews, or meat that's been cooked on a barbecue. Shiraz can take even more spice.

Italian reds e.g. Barolo, Chianti Always best enjoyed with classic Italian food, preferably from the region. Barolo is particularly good with braised beef, game, rich pasta and truffles. Chianti shines with Italian-style roast lamb and veal and with baked pasta dishes.

Rioja and other Spanish reds Spanish reds are changing fast. The typical style used to be exemplified by Rioja Reservas and Gran Reservas with their soft, delicate fruit and gentle tannins (good with grilled lamb, game, sheeps' cheeses and subtly spiced stews and tagines), but the new wave of reds can handle much more robust flavours, more like a Cabernet Sauvignon.

Zinfandel, Pinotage and other rustic reds These are ideal for your heartiest meals like big rich meaty stews and braises.

SWEET WINES

Top dessert wines like Sauternes are at their best with simple fruit tarts, especially apple, pear, peach or nectarine-based ones and strawberry tarts with crème pâtissière (cream helps to show off sweet wines). You can also drink them with rich liver pâtés and with blue cheese (the latter also being the classic way to enjoy vintage port).

CHAMPAGNE

Champagne is a surprisingly flexible partner for food, particularly eggs and seafood, and also handles Chinese and Japanese food well. A glass of sweet (demi-sec) Champagne is also a glamorous way to finish off a special meal – it goes well with gâteaux and celebration cakes.

Frequently asked questions

What sort of wine glasses do I need?
Ideally, it's useful to have four different types – a generously sized wine glass for red wines, a smaller one for white wines, a set of tall Champagne flutes and a set of small glasses for sherry, port and dessert wines.

How long do I need to chill wine for?
It depends on the wine. Most people tend to serve white wines too cold and red wines too warm. Champagne and dessert wines need chilling longest (about 1½–2 hours, depending on the temperature of your fridge), crisp dry whites need about about 1–1½ hours, full-bodied whites and light reds about 45 minutes to an hour. Even full-bodied reds benefit from being served cool rather than at room temperature (about 15–18°C), so keep them in a cooler area before serving.

How much wine should you pour in a glass?
Don't fill it more than two-thirds full. Not out of meanness, but so that you can appreciate its aromas.

How long before the meal should I open red wine?
Its only worth opening them ahead if you're going to decant them. Otherwise not much air can get into the bottle. Most wines are designed to be drunk direct from the bottle these days.

When should I decant a wine?
Only when it's very full bodied and tannic or has thrown a deposit like vintage port. Be careful about decanting older reds. If they're very old and fragile, they may lose their delicate flavours when exposed to air.

How do I decant a bottle of wine?
Leave the bottle upright for at least 24 hours before you plan to serve it (so that any deposit can settle). Then, with a light behind the neck of the bottle, pour slowly and steadily into the decanter without stopping until you see the sediment inch towards the neck of the bottle.

How do I tell if a wine is corked?
If it tastes musty or stale, there almost certainly is something wrong with it and you're perfectly within your rights to reject it (so long as you don't drink half the bottle first!). If it's simply too sweet or too sharp for your taste, then you've got no real grounds to send it back. The grey area is with older wines or ones made from less common grape varieties, which may have funky flavours that aren't to your taste. But if a supplier or restaurant values your goodwill, they will replace it.

Should you open the wine your guests have brought?
The trickiest issue I find! It depends how it's presented. If they bring along an unchilled bottle of Champagne, I think it's fair to accept that it is intended as a private treat to enjoy on another occasion. If they produce a bottle that they're clearly excited about, the indications are that they want to share it with you.

If I'm invited to dinner should I take a bottle and, if so, what type? It depends how well you know your hosts. If you don't know them well, you don't want to imply that they won't serve you a decent bottle, so it's better to take something indulgent like a bottle of Champagne or a special dessert wine that could be construed as a gift. With good friends it's fine to ask what they'd like you to bring or what they're making so that you can choose something appropriate.

Index

Credits

Photography

Key: ph= photographer, a=above,
b=below, r=right, l=left, c=centre.

Jan Baldwin: Page 126

Peter Cassidy: Pages 9, 16ar, 16cr,
17, 27c, 32r, 38, 45, 52, 64–67, 68,
71, 74–75, 78–81, 90, 93ar, 97b, 98,
99, 106, 109, 113, 115, 125, 130, 137,
141, 144a all, 151r, 154–155, 159r, 161,
164–165, 178, 180

David Brittain: Pages 15bl, 18–21,
24ac, &br

Dan Duchars: Page 35bl

Jonathan Gregson: Pages 29–31, 32l,
33, 35a both, 35br, 36–37, 39, 40al&br,
42–44, 46–47, 101

Richard Jung: Pages 14, 16bc, 53, 54,
82–83, 150l, 152–153, 162–163

William Lingwood: Pages 166, 168-
171, 172a, 173, 176-177

Paul Massey: Page 114l cushion
designed by Jan Constantine
(www.janconstantine.com)

Claire Richardson: Page 172b

Debi Treloar: Pages 6, 8, 11, 12a all,
12b all, 12cr, 15a all, 15c all, 15br,
16al, ac, cl, c & bl, 23all, 24al, 24ar,
24c, 24cr both, 24bl, 27a all, 27cl&cr,
27b all, 28, 40ar&bl, 86a, 108, 151l,
159l

Kate Whitaker: Endpapers, Pages 1–3,
10, 25, 48–51, 56–63, 69–70, 72, 73,
76–77, 84–85, 86b, 87-89, 91, 93al &
b, 94, 96, 97a, 100, 102–105, 107,
110–112, 114r, 116, 117, 120–124,
127–129, 131–135, 138–140, 142, 143,
144b, 145–148, 150r, 156–158, 160,
167, 174, 175, 185–187

Polly Wreford: Pages 4–5, 12 c & cl,
16br, 24cl

Recipes and text

Liz Belton
Setting the Scene (chapter)

Emily Chalmers
How to set a table

Fiona Beckett
Secrets of successful entertaining
(introduction)
Wine with food (chapter)
Apricot tart with Muscat de
Beaumes-de-Venise
Boeuf bourguignon with pomme purée
Charcuterie and radishes
Chicken, lemon and green olive
tagine
Chocolates, coffee and cognac
Deli-bought tapas
Farmer's market salad with goats'
cheese, asparagus and roast beetroot
Grape and lemon mascarpone tart
Heirloom tomato, pepper and
mozzarella tart
Lobster and chips
Mexican tostaditas
Passion fruit pavlovas
Pork and olive empanadas
Prawn and cucumber sesame noodles
Pumpkin soup with honey and sage
Seared tuna with tomatoes, rocket and
gremolata
Seasonal cheeseboards
Smoked salmon kedgeree
Sparkling shiraz and summer berry
jellies
Spring vegetable pasta with lemon
Strawberry tiramisu
Thai-style beef with tomato and
herb salad

Tonia George
Bircher muesli
Blood orange and Campari mimosa
Bloody Mary
Blueberry pancakes
Cheesy polenta with sausages and
red onions
Eggs Benedict
Exploding berry crumble muffins
Garlic mushrooms and goats' cheese
on sourdough toast
Granola, nectarine and ricotta parfait
Hot smoked salmon hash with dill
crème fraîche
Linguine with lemon, basil and
Parmesan cream
Nutty honey granola
Potato and rosemary pancakes with
bacon and honey
Reubens with beef, sauerkraut
and Emmenthal
Scrambled eggs with smoked trout
and shiso

Sea breeze
Steak and fried egg baps with
mustard butter
Sugary jam doughnut muffins
Sweet potato pancakes with hot
smoked trout and chilli-lime butter

Ross Dobson
Affogato parfait
Baked cheesecake
Baked chipolatas in tomato and basil
sauce on soft polenta
Baked salmon with chilli and
fresh herbs
Beef daube
Blueberry madeleines with little
lemon creams
Brined roast chicken with a ham
and fresh sage stuffing
Cherry and walnut brownies
Chicken pot pies
Chilli salt squid
Chocolate marquise
Chocolate orange mousse
Chocolate truffles
Coq au leftover red wine
Flan casero
Foraged mushroom risotto
Fresh mussels with fennel aïoli
Fresh raspberry and almond tart
Fresh tomato, pea and paneer curry
Garlic-infused olive oil, warm
marinated olives with Serrano ham
Gnocchetti pasta with smoky chorizo
and seared prawns
Greek salad with butter beans
Home-made potato gnocchi with
roasted tomato sauce
Houmous
Keralan prawn curry
Lamb kefta with crunchy salad
Lemon harissa chicken with
oven-roasted vegetables
Linguine with garlic and chilli clams
Messy strawberries Romanoff
Moroccan-style white fish, potato and
tomato tagine
Mushroom, spinach and potato bake
Pappardelle pasta with roast fennel,
tomato and olives
Parmesan biscuits
Pasta salad with tuna, chilli and rocket
Pear, almond and mascarpone tart
Polenta chips with green Tabasco
mayonnaise
Pork and chicken liver terrine
Pork sausage, fennel and haricot
bean stew
Potato crisps with soured cream and
caviar dip
Quick chilli meatballs with penne
Rhubarb and custard pots
Roast beef rib-eye with café de Paris
butter and asparagus
Roast chicken and minted tabbouleh
salad

Roast ducklings with orange and
ginger pilaf
Roast turkey breast with olive
salsa verde
Roasted hazelnut and chocolate cake
Roasted red pepper and walnut dip
Roasted tomato soup with rarebit toasts
Rosemary risotto with roasted
summer vegetables
Salmon rillettes with Melba toast
Sesame prawn toasts with pickled carrot
Shepherd's pie
Shoulder of lamb with oven-roasted
vegetables
Slow-cooked lamb shanks in red wine
with white beans
Slow-cooked spiced pork belly with
apple and fennel
Slow-cooked tomatoes with goats'
cheese and garlic toasts
Smoked trout fattoush
Smoked trout, celeriac and apple salad
Snapper pie
Soft goats' cheese and fennel tart
Spiced Muscat figs
Spicy Cajun mixed nuts
Spicy chilli bean dip
Spicy pork curry with lemon rice
Stuffed giant mushrooms with feta
and herbs
Summer fruit compote with zabaglione
Sweet potato and coconut soup with
Thai pesto
Thai-style fish with smoky tomato
relish
Toasted mozzarella and basil fingers
Trio of vegetable dips with spelt toasts
Truffled egg linguine
Vietnamese chicken curry
White chocolate pots
Za-atar salmon with lentil salad

Louise Pickford
Bagels with smoked salmon and
wasabi crème fraîche

Ben Reed
Cosmopolitan
Kir royale
Margarita
Martini
Mojito
Negroni
Original daiquiri
Perfect Manhattan
Sidecar